The American Taxi

A Century of Service

Ben Merkel and Chris Monier

Iconografix

Iconografix
PO Box 446
Hudson, Wisconsin 54016 USA

Library of Congress Control Number: 2006926933

ISBN-13: 978-1-58388-176-7
ISBN-10: 1-58388-176-X

06 07 08 09 10 11 6 5 4 3 2 1

Printed in China

Cover and book design by Dan Perry

Copyedited by Suzie Helberg

On the cover: Shown are a 1930 Studebaker, a 1946 DeSoto Skyview and a 2002 Ford Crown Victoria.

Book Proposals

Iconografix is a publishing company specializing in books for transportation enthusiasts. We publish in a number of different areas, including Automobiles, Auto Racing, Buses, Construction Equipment, Emergency Equipment, Farming Equipment, Railroads & Trucks. The Iconografix imprint is constantly growing and expanding into new subject areas.

Authors, editors, and knowledgeable enthusiasts in the field of transportation history are invited to contact the Editorial Department at Iconografix, Inc., PO Box 446, Hudson, WI 54016.

Acknowledgments

Nathan Willensky
Henry Winningham
Alma & Alvaro Gallego
Michael Angelich
Bobby Lowich
Linda Danzig at National Taxicab Supply company
Ernest Aguilar & Patty Leon at Lancaster Uniform Cap Co.
Roger & Linda Lamm
George L. Hamlin and the Packard club of America
Bob Zimmerman
Charles Ledbetter at Cabometer, Inc.
Patty & Louie Ghilarducci
Richard Headley, United Garage, Cleveland
Claude Brami
Frédéric Robert
Claude Lefebvre
Paul Belanger
Joe Fay and the Checker Car Club of America
Peter Yanello
Bruce A. Uhrich
John Iannuzzi
Monte Conner
Richard De Luna
Joe Pollard
Alyn Thomas, Manning Brothers Photography, Detroit
Barbera Thompson, Detroit Public Library
Tami Suzuki, San Francisco Public Library
San Francisco Yellow Cab Company
Charles & Nathalie Tissier
Brooklin Models
Lars Wennerqvist
Kathryn Bassett
Henry and Tom Merkel
Bob Hinkley
Diane and Roger Slagle
The Walt Disney company
Jacques Daniel
Brandt Rosenbush at DaimlerChrysler Historical collection
Jim Fox
Amishi Sandesara, Corbis
Gilmore Museum
Auburn-Cord-Duesenberg Museum
Peter Kanze

And especially to those who have had to co-exist with old taxis and their related memorabilia for many years:
Chris' beloved wife Leah, children Gavin, Cheyenne and Curtis, and Ben's sons Matthew and Ian.

If we have inadvertently neglected to mention a contributor, our profoundest apologies.

Bibliography

Angelich, Michael, "The K2 Checker," *The Checkerboard News*, 2004

Butler, Don, "The Plymouth-DeSoto Story," Crestline Publishing, 1978

Coachbult website: coachbult.com

"Checker UtilityVehicle Is Truck or Passenger Car," *Automobile Topics*, August 1931

Francis, Edward & DeAngelis, George, *Model A News*, July-August 1974

Gilbert, Gorman & Samuels, Robert E, THE TAXICAB, AN URBAN TRANSPORTATION SURVIVOR, The University of North Carolina Press, 1982

Georgano, George N, "The Taxi Project," The New York Museum of Modern Art, 1976

Gonzalez Jr, A.F., "That The US Needs: A Taxi Like London's," *Boston Globe*, 08/19/1974

Gunnell, John A., *The Standard Catalog of American Cars 1946-1975*, Krause Publications, 1992

Hamlin, George, *The Packard Cormorant*, The Packard Club of America

Heasley, Jerry, *The Production Figure Book for US Cars*, 1977

Hogg, Tony, "Is The London Cab The Answer?" *Road and Track magazine*, 08/68

Kowalke, Ron, *The Standard Catalog of Independents*, Krause Publications, 1999

Maloney, James, *Studebaker Cars,* Crestline Publishing, 1994

"New British Diesel Taxicab to be Used Here by Checker," *Detroit News*, 11/22/1959

Scrimger, D.L., *Taxicab Scrapbook*, D.L. Scrimger, 1979

Seltzer, Bob, The Cleveland Press, 11/18/1959

"The 1962 Taxicab," Taxicab Industry/*Auto Rental News*, 11/1961

Watts, Ralph B, "Taxicab Owners Study Compacts," *Detroit News,* 12/3/1960

Winningham, Henry, *The Checker Cab Manufacturing Story* and *The Yellow Cab Manufacturing Story*, currently unpublished

Yost, Stanley & Bassett, Kathryn, "Taxi ! A Look At Checker's Past," Misc. Enterprises, 1990

Foreword

By Robbie Coltrane, British Actor and Auto Enthusiast

I first saw a Checker Cab, (or should that be a host of Golden Checkers?), at JFK Airport sometime in the Seventies. Disco was huge, and I wasn't!

Having been brought up with the Black Cab, or Hackney Carriage as it is properly called, that London Icon with its tiny turning circle and clattery wee diesel engine, you have to imagine a young man with his Scottish eyes out on stalks, as he was dazzled by a sea of bright yellow steel.

It was love at first sight. To a European eye, the Checker looked like every childs' drawing of an American Car! Big and bold and very business-like. It took time, over the next year or two, to appreciate the very subtle proportions of the Checker; it's hard to imagine that changing one part of the design could in any way improve it, the measure, surely, of a Classic. As your eye travels along, from the impressive girder that acts as a bumper up front, to the elegant trunk, flanked by the silver plates that carry the elegant red lamps at the rear, the lines are as pure as any car costing ten, fifteen times as much. Trust me, I have a Bentley.

To sit in the back is a joy; there is so much room, both at your feet, and above your head. The visibility is excellent; for a New Boy in Town, this was the way to see Manhattan, as we cruised the Mid Town Bridge! I decided there

and then, I would have to own one of these beauties. As I could only just pay the fare at the time, this seemed as likely as Debbie Harry asking me to marry her, another fantasy I nurtured at the time.

My dream came true some years ago, and I now know what it feels like to sit in the excellent driving position, hear the Chevy small-block hum as it pulls the cab up winding, mountainous roads in Scotland. (Debbie never did call, by the way, but I got over it.)

Don't get me wrong, my view isn't entirely romantic; driving a cab to pay the rent is a demanding, tiring, and sometimes even dangerous way to go. I did it a long time ago, as a gypsy driver.

My lasting memory of the "working" Checker would be at the decline of her glory days in New York. Much to the irritation of my girlfriend at the time, I would be standing in the pouring rain outside some Club in Manhattan, letting all the Ford cabs go by till a Checker would appear out of the gloom, flagging it down, slipping through that huge door, sliding into the soft bench seat, and heading home.

Now the Checker is an old friend, my kids love the fact they can get all their pals in, and I like the idea that she will be running long after I am.

Enjoy this book, I know I shall!
Robbie Coltrane, 2006

Introduction

An American taxicab's life is not complicated: It starts out factory fresh and, after a few years and several hundred thousand miles, becomes wretched and disgusting. While some of the better examples might get sold to employees or other cab companies, most are quietly shuffled off to the boneyard with nary an insurance photo to remember them by. The public has wisely avoided buying decommissioned taxis as private transportation because the old moneymakers have a well-deserved reputation for being problematic, no matter what the brand or year. This understandable lack of interest in the old relics has resulted in a very poor survival rate for all taxis more than 20 years old and many are only seen in period movies, magazines, and postcards.

Old cabs are generally pretty nasty automobiles. Typically, decals, signage, radios, and meters are hastily removed, leaving behind hanging wires, numerous dash holes, and blotches of missing exterior paint. Many operators will stop doing routine maintenance in advance of a cab's imminent retirement so mechanicals are frequently wanting. Good batteries, tires, and hubcaps are almost always removed and replaced with marginal stand-ins for what is supposed to be the last ride to the recycler's yard. To make things even more unappetizing for those wanting to take an ex-cab home, most taxis built since the mid 1950s were stripped down, four-door sedans with interiors as glamorous as a utility shower.

There is little room for nostalgia within the taxi industry. Most cab companies are situated near metropolitan areas where land is expensive and space is at a premium. Keeping a classic, old cab in a corner of the taxi repair garage is a common fantasy among operators but few have the room for such indulgences. Indoor shelf space can also become precious and old taxi accouterments, like obsolete roof lights and meters, can easily wind up being thrown out. Operators are in the business of making money and if something isn't making money or it's not a part of the income process, it probably doesn't need to be around. Frequently, taxicab history is confined to a few old pictures hanging on a wall, some employee recollections, and maybe a mechanical meter or two. Real antique taxis, the ones that really were used as cabs, are very rare or non-existent today. Many enthusiasts have taken civilian cars and painted them to look like taxis because the real thing is generally not available.

Since a yellow paint job is about the only thing keeping any car from being a taxi, it's probably safe to say that nearly every domestic sedan ever built has been pressed into for-hire service at some time or another and even high-end luxury cars are not immune from the call of the street once they are a few years old. There is no shame in generating high mileage because only the toughest cars can take the punishment dished out by America's urban taxi drivers. Like airliners, buses, and trains, taxis take us to destinations for money and then we have the luxury of forgetting about them because they generally do their jobs so well. Major design changes can momentarily shock the traveling public into noticing new equipment but, after a couple of rides in the new animal, the novelty wears off and that blissful indifference sets in again.

This book is an introduction to the world of taxicabs and it photographically chronicles the evolution of the American motorized taxi from its humble beginnings as electric hansom cabs to the current gas/electric hybrid SUVs currently appearing on both coasts. The ins and outs of the taxi industry itself have been documented elsewhere so the focus here is primarily on the cars themselves and the builders of these machines. We have tried to be accurate but information pertaining to some of the old cabs and their related memorabilia is vague or currently unknown. Many of the brands of taxis shown in this book are there because we happened to have pictures or brochures of them. Not surprisingly, Checker and DeSoto get a lot of air time for the simple reason that they were both major players in the largest taxi markets in the States: New York City, Chicago, and Los Angeles. Arguably, the boxy 1956 to 1982 Checker is the most famous taxi of the 20th century simply because it was in production so long that three generations of Americans had the chance to grow up with it. Cleveland, Ohio's United Garage is well represented because they are the local, big city cab company and have been documented regularly. Some pictures were provided with no labels or turned up in multiple copies so there is no way to realistically determine whom the original photographer was and a misidentified photo could be possible under these circumstances.

The study, preservation, and enjoyment of old cabs has been a source of great entertainment for a few individuals calling themselves taxi enthusiasts—persons for whom every airport or downtown area is rife with potential subject material. If we can pass some of this interest to the reader, then we have accomplished our mission.

1897 to 1929

The motorized taxicab can trace its recorded ancestry back to about 4,000 B.C. when Egyptian boats carried persons up and down the Nile River, presumably for an agreed upon fee. In Roman times, hired chariots kept track of distances traveled with small stones dropped every so many paces. More recently, during the 17th century, specialized horse-drawn conveyances, known as hackney coaches, appeared in Paris and London to transport the upper crust of society around these growing urban centers. The word "hackney" itself is derived from the French word, "haquenée," meaning a strong horse that ambles with a comfortable gait, thereby giving riders a relatively smooth trip. The shortened slang version, "hack," is still used today to describe a taxicab. The typical coach was a two-passenger vehicle pulled by two horses and, like today, cabbies frequently waited for passengers at stands situated outside of transportation centers and major hotels.

In Paris around 1800 A.D., the hackney coach evolved into a fast, one passenger, two wheeled unit pulled by a single horse. They were called "cabriolets," a name that was quickly shortened to the familiar "cab" we know so well. Englishman Joseph Hansom introduced a further improvement in 1834 when he designed a two-passenger vehicle

Joseph Hansom, an English architect, designed a two-wheeled cab with space for two passengers inside while the driver rode on top. Hansom sold the patent rights in 1836 to John Chapman, a London taxi operator, who improved the hansom cab by moving the driver to the rear for better weight distribution. A trap door in the roof allowed the driver to converse with the passengers. There were quite a few imitators but generally they were all called "hansom cabs" no matter what company manufactured them. *Chris Monier*

The first motorized cabs in the United States were electric vehicles produced by Harry G. Morris and Pedro G. Salom of Philadelphia in 1896. These revolutionary cabs, known as "Electrobats," were put on the streets of Philadelphia later that year and 12 were put into service in New York City the following January. At least 800 lbs of batteries were under the driver's seat towards the rear and the large front wheels provided the movement while the smaller rear wheels steered. Maximum speed was about 15 mph and range was limited by the battery technology at the time. Recharging took eight hours. Two Electrobats are shown in front of the old Philadelphia Opera House on 39th Street in 1898. *Nathan Willensky*

In 1897, the rights to build the Electrobat were acquired by the Electric Vehicle Company of Elizabethtown, New Jersey, which made new electric taxis in Hartford, Connecticut, under the Columbia name. At this time all four tires were changed to the same size. The front wheels had large, inner gear sprockets that were powered by small gears attached to electric motors. The driver's controls appeared basic with a lever next to the operator's seat that controlled forward and reverse, a hinged tiller in the middle for steering, and what looked to be a brake pedal in the floor. The driver could communicate with fares via a trap door located on top of the passenger compartment. Columbia ceased production of electric taxis by 1905. This Electrobat, with the number 937 etched on its coach light lens, was one of 200 electric taxis serving Manhattan in 1900. *Detroit Public Library*

where the driver sat outside and the pampered passengers rode inside. In 1836, Hansom sold his patented design to a London cab operator, John Chapman, who continued the basic idea but made his own changes in the interests of evolution. Despite the new features introduced by Chapman, the name "hansom cab" had become a generic term not only for his own products but also for any two-wheeled cab with a similar layout. New York City received its first hansom cabs in 1890.

A major innovation occurred in 1891 when a German named Wilhelm Bruhn invented a device that accurately measured the distance travelled so the customer was mechanically charged a proper fare. The word "taximeter" is a combination of the French word "taxe," meaning price, and the Greek term "metron," or measure. Early cabbies weren't too thrilled at the prospect of objective fares so they tossed Bruhn into the Frankfurt-am-Main River as a protest. While the inventor may have gotten all wet, his invention and the term "taximeter" have persevered to this day.

The American hansom cabs became electric with the introduction of the 1896 Electrobats in Philadelphia and Manhattan the following year. Top speed was about 15 mph and cruising range was limited by the battery technology of the time. Overseas, the first motorized taxicab race took place in Paris in June 1898 and consisted of 14 entrants, all electric except for one gasoline-engined Peugeot. The Peugeot's ability to put on speed without reducing its range was a big plus but, when compared to the smooth, quiet electrics, it appeared noisy, smelly, and rough running to potential operators. Almost 10 years would pass before the gasoline engine had improved enough to surpass the electrics. Not surprisingly, the first gasoline taxis that appeared in New York City and Chicago circa 1907 were French cabs, mostly Darracqs, Renaults, and Unics. A New Yorker named Harry N. Allen coined the word "taxicab" when he introduced 65 new Darracqs, each equipped with a meter, onto the streets of Manhattan. The name of his new company was the New York Taxicab Association.

It was also during this era that the driver, previously left out in the elements, was beginning to enjoy a roof over the operator's seat. Due to the big difference in social status between operators and fares, creature comforts for the poor devil behind the wheel had never been a priority in cab design. For most of recorded history, paid rides were mostly the bastion of the well to do and commingling between passengers and cabbies was minimal. Even after the driver's seat was made a proper part of the interior in the early 1920s, a privacy partition almost always existed between the front seat and the rear compartment until the mid 1950s. To make sure no fares could sit up front, a generally uncomfortable bucket seat precluded even the possibility of a rider by earmarking the open space next to the driver for luggage only. In many cities, the law required a bucket seat and partition along with fancy uniforms with brass buttons and big, shiny boots. Operators carefully cultivated the image of the cab driver as a true gentleman who was ready to open the door for you and fluff up the rear leather seat with a wooden paddle. Some fleets allowed only married men to get behind the wheel.

As the 20th century progressed, more and more automakers got into the cab manufacturing business since it was pretty much a wide-open field and anybody could play. Regulations were few and, since the average American could now afford to take a taxi, the growth of the industry was explosive. In January 1924, Chicago hosted the first ever taxi exhibit show with Reo, Mogul-Checker, Willys-Knight, Overland, Premier, Pennant, Dodge, Rauch & Lang, and Roamer taxis all represented, some with elaborate displays showing cut-away cars. In New York City from 1925 to 1928, there were no fewer than 25 different brands of taxis operating compared to the two heavy hitters found there today. Since cars were still framed in wood, endless body style variations were possible and a lot of stock automobile chassis were fitted with special taxi bodies from a myriad of coachbuilders.

The domestic automobile improved a lot during the

1920s with the addition of safety glass, four-wheel hydraulic brakes, better tires, and superior drivetrain components. In terms of overall performance, there was no comparison between a 1919 taxi and its 1929 counterpart. Modern production techniques brought the price of a new car down to the point where it was within the financial grasp of the burgeoning middle class and, as a result, private vehicle ownership increased tremendously from 1910 to 1930, thanks in part to Ford's Model T. Taxi ridership was largely unaffected by the public's new mobility because many of the fresh, urban dwellers in America's fastest growing cities couldn't afford a car and would be unable to purchase one until after World War II. In New York City, where there wasn't a limit on the number of taxis and no regulations regarding a driver's qualifications, the number of cabs skyrocketed to 30,000 by 1930, over double the number working there today. While all this was well and good, the coming economic downturn of 1929 would cause chaos to reign within the taxi industry.

In 1907, a man named Harry N. Allen was grossly overcharged by a Manhattan cab driver for a short ride. Mr. Allen was infuriated by the event and vowed to open up his own cab company with rates that were mechanically metered and not subject to a driver's whim. He orchestrated the purchase of 65 new, red French Darracq taxis, each equipped with a meter, and put them to work at his own arranged cab stands at major hotels. Allen combined the French word "taxi-metre" and the shortened version of "cabriolet" to coin the word "taxicab." By 1908, his company had grown to 700 cabs. Here's what a row of Darracq taxis looked like in front of the old Hotel Marlborough in New York City. The steering wheel was on the right side and the meter was mounted on the left front roof post. Note the almost whimsical roof extension over the driver. *Detroit Public Library*

The passenger in this turn-of-the-century electric taxi of unknown manufacture demonstrated the huge disparity in social status between drivers and their generally well-to-do passengers. Not only was there no physical sharing of the same area but also the operator had to sit up on top, exposed to the elements. About the only plus for the driver was that the relatively pampered fare arrived at accidents sooner. This taxi used a chain to rotate the front wheels. By 1910, with advancements in gasoline technologies, electrics were on the way out. *Nathan Willensky*

A 1909 Overland Model 31 taxi with collapsible rear roof section was priced out at a fairly hefty $1,500 with a four-cylinder motor rated at 30 horsepower. Several items of interest include the steamer trunk on the driver's left. On a hard right turn, it looks as if there was nothing holding it in place except the driver's quick reflexes. An acetylene tank on the running board provided fuel for the headlights. All of the shades were pulled down in the rear compartment so that the passenger could travel incognito. *Nathan Willensky*

A row of new 1909 Kayton Taxis line up outside of the Kayton Taxicab and Garage Company in New York City. Note the large "K" on the front grille. *Detroit Public Library*

It is believed that Rockwell Motor Car built taxis from 1908 to 1911 in Bristol, Connecticut. Here a 1910 example is shown with a very dour looking driver. The meter was mounted outside on the right, middle doorpost over the luggage area, which had a little fence to keep baggage from slipping away. The driver was wearing typical operator's garb for the time: a giant fur coat. Rockwell taxis were used in Manhattan and Chicago. *Detroit Public Library*

The White Motor Company of Cleveland, Ohio, offered taxis on two different chassis: the GA car chassis, shown here, or on a GB 3/4-ton truck chassis with similar body design. This 1913 or 1914 Model GA Type was one of 14 in service with the Wall Street Cab Company in New York City and it featured a convertible roof over the last seat. The driver had a two-piece windshield where the top and bottom portions could swing up for ventilation. The motor was a 30-hp, 226-ci, four-cylinder White Motor Company engine with a four-speed transmission. The Theodore Kundtz Company in Cleveland, a major, top quality builder of furniture, cabinets, and auto bodies, built the taxi body locally. *Henry Merkel*

John D. Hertz

John D. Hertz, born April 10, 1879, came to Chicago at an early age from the small town of Ruttka, Austria. After a tough childhood and several jobs as a newspaper copy boy, truck driver, and sports writer, Hertz found, in 1905, that he was good at selling French automobiles for a man by the name of Walden W. Shaw. For $2,000 Hertz became a one-quarter partner in the W. W. Shaw Livery Company in 1908. As sales increased, a lot of trade-ins caused Hertz to put the used cars to work as taxicabs. This is how Hertz fell into the taxi business. In 1910, after experimenting with 12 different used cars, the Shaw Company purchased nine new, yellow Thomas Flyers for use as cabs. Yellow with a hint of red was the color chosen because it proved to be the most visible at long distances, according to University of Chicago testing.

By 1915, Hertz had complete control of the Shaw Company and was supervising the building of their own cabs at the livery company's garage just off 25th and South Park Avenue in Chicago. The first cars were Model J Yellow Cabs and they had as their radiator ornament a round emblem with a "Y" in the middle. The three sections formed by this "Y" represented the three branches of the Chicago River. By 1916, Yellow brand taxis were operating in six major cities and had become one of the largest cab producers in the US. The name of the company was changed around this time to Yellow Cab Manufacturing Company. By 1925, Yellow was the biggest taxi manufacturer in the world.

Hertz had definite ideas about how a taxicab company should be run and he kept high standards for his drivers. Every driver had to be bonded, married, and was required to wear a fancy uniform with brass buttons. Before each shift, a driver would have to present himself to the dispatcher for approval. To increase efficiency, Hertz installed call boxes at strategic locations around the city to minimize the need for drivers to return to the cab company empty for their next call order.

In 1923, Hertz bought out a 600-car rental agency in Chicago as a market for his newest venture, a modified version of the Yellow taxi called the "Hertz" car. The Yellow Drive-It-Yourself Company was started in 1924 but the concept received a lukewarm reception, as most car renters didn't want to be seen in a vehicle that was clearly a rental and not possibly their own. In 1925, Hertz sold Yellow Cab Manufacturing and Yellow Drive-It-Yourself to General Motors so he could pursue other endeavors. General Motors built Yellow brand taxis up until 1929 when they dropped the Yellow name and began calling their taxis "Generals" in 1930. In 1953, General Motors sold Yellow Drive-It-Yourself back to Hertz's Omnibus Corporation for $10.8 million and the name was changed to Hertz Rent-A-Car.

John D. Hertz served on the Board of Directors at Hertz Rent-A-Car for one year before retiring in 1955 and passing away in 1961. In 2005, Ford Motor Company paid $6 billion for Hertz Rent-A-Car.

A new 1916 Yellow Cab Model J was one of 300 ready to go to work in New York City for the Black and White Cab Company. Since Yellow Cab Manufacturing of Chicago owned it, it shared the same basic logo as Chicago Yellow Cab, which was a round belt with a "Y" in the middle. This Yellow had a hand-operated spotlight and a round Jones Taximeter. In 1919 Black and White switched to large 36-lb Ohmer meters that printed receipts. *Nathan Willensky*

1916 Yellow Cab Newspaper ad showing a driver putting tire chains. *1916 Chicago Newspaper ad*

An earnest driver looked poised to make some money in Detroit, Michigan, driving this 1917 Yellow Model K Cab. The rear door had a cloverleaf logo that read "Yellow Taxicab Company." The company's phone number, "Cadillac 3333," was put into the top of a belt-shaped logo, which meant the cab was part of the Chicago-based Yellow Cab Manufacturing Corporation. The operator had access to a manual horn mounted on top of the driver's door but there were no snaps to indicate that there was any driver protection in the winter. January and February must have been long months for hearty Detroit cabbies. All Yellows were powered by a Continental four-cylinder and came with Firestone tires as standard equipment. This particular Detroit Yellow featured tires that were painted white and two spares. *Manning Brothers*

Yellow Cab Manufacturing fashioned interiors in leather with washable door panels and scuff plates along the floor. The jump seats came out of the partition and faced rearward allowing room for five behind the partition. *Manning Brothers*

Detroit's Yellow Cab Company was still using Yellow Cab to manufacture taxis in 1919, and this one, Number 102, was parked outside of the cab garage in 1923 after four years of service. Since 1917, Detroit Yellow had switched to the optional spoked wheels and dropped the belt logo in favor of standard "Yellow Cab" lettering. The coach lights, as seen on the 1917 Detroit Yellow Cab, were replaced around 1918 by lights on the cowl. Spoked wheels remained as an option for another year or two and then they, too, vanished. *Manning Brothers*

The Briggs Manufacturing Corporation of Detroit, Michigan, got its first big break in 1910 with an order for Ford Model T interiors. Eleven years later they were building custom taxi bodies for the same car as this 1921 Model T picture shows. The rear roof was collapsible and a partition, probably with at least one jump seat, existed between the driver and the fares in back. The operator had a roof but no side windows. *Manning Brothers*

One of two remaining from 1922 to 1923 production, this 1923 Checker Model E belongs to the company that created it, Checker Motors Corporation. Powered by a four-cylinder motor made by the Buda Engine Company of Chicago, it has a three-speed manual transmission with brakes on the rear wheels. For a healthy $2,500, standard equipment included tools, jack, horn, spare wheel and carrier, spotlight, heater, and dome light in a cab with five-passenger capacity in back. While they were much more expensive than cheaper cabs, the built-for-the-purpose Checkers and Yellows would last a lot longer under severe, big city conditions. *Joe Fay*

Morris Markin

Morris Markin

Checker Motors' Morris Markin was born in Smolensk, Russia, in 1893 and he immigrated to the United States at the age of 19 after spending some years at a clothing factory. He went to work for his uncle in Chicago and learned the tailoring business from him. World War I found Markin prospering with military contracts at his newly formed pants factory and this fresh funding was, ironically, the catalyst for inadvertently getting him into the cab making business.

The ball began rolling in 1921 when a $15,000 loan by Markin to a taxi body manufacturer named Lomberg got shaky and Markin, in an effort to protect his investment, took over Lomberg's operation and renamed it Markin Auto Body Corporation. At the same time another company engaged in the building of taxicab chassis called Commonwealth Motors was on the financial ropes, too, so Markin wisely put the two needy companies together and created the Checker Cab Manufacturing Company in 1922. It is thought that the name "Checker" was chosen since Commonwealth Motors had a contract to produce chassis for Chicago's Checker Cab Company.

Checker's first car, the Model C, was produced in Joliet, Illinois, in early 1922 and was a contemporary, boxy vehicle that looked very much like its competitors. With orders beginning to flow in, the Joliet factory was proving

too small so Markin moved the operation to Kalamazoo, Michigan, and took over the recently vacated Handly-Knight and Dort Body buildings on North Pitcher Street, where Checker still calls home today.

Since he was now in the cab making business, Markin's next logical step was to get into taxi operations, thus providing a ready market for his own vehicles. This process began in 1929 with the creation of National Transportation Company in New York City, a firm that would eventually operate 1,500 cabs in Manhattan alone. Next, he purchased Chicago's Parmelee Transportation, a railway shuttle service that owned a 30-percent share of Chicago Yellow Cab, the largest cab company in the world. In 1935, he and several associates took control of Chicago Checker Cab, the third largest taxi fleet at that time. Markin also controlled the Yellow Cab companies in Pittsburg, Cleveland, and Minneapolis. Altogether, these fleets were tremendous outlets for his own products and allowed Checker Cab Manufacturing to survive.

Morris Markin passed away in 1970 but the company he founded is still in business and still in family hands today. Since the production of its famous taxi ended on July 12, 1982, Checker Motors has concentrated on its metal stamping operations and currently supplies parts to the major automakers.

A row of 1923 Checkers came out of the factory in Kalamazoo, Michigan, for delivery to a Deluxe Cab Company. The "For Hire" sign in the windshield was a common requirement in many cities until at least the late 1930s. The small, rectangular roof light said "Deluxe" on it. *Ben Merkel*

1923 Checker Mogul fleet view - *Henry Winningham*

Francis O. French, a former millionaire and distant relative to William H. Vanderbilt, began his new career as a Mogul-Checker driver in New York City around 1924. Along with the Mogul-Checker uniform, he had a manually operated horn mounted on the driver's door as well as a spotlight on the left windshield pillar for illuminating addresses at night. The Mogul-Checker Cab Sales Company was created in 1923 to help Checker sell and service taxis in the New York City market. *Henry Winningham*

A 1922 or 1923 Yellow Model 03 taxi was in service in the San Francisco, California, area and showed off something that Checker Cab Manufacturing wouldn't allow in Chicago after 1923 nor would New York City the following year: checkerboards on anything other than one of their cabs. If any operator tried to use checkerboards in those cities, they surely expected a legal threat from Checker Cab Manufacturing over trademark infringement. Conversely, the name "Yellow" has been in the public domain for a long time and there are no restrictions on who can use it. Yellows, like this one photographed in 1926, were still powered by Continental four-cylinders. *San Francisco Public Library*

The reason why taxi bodies from this time period look so much alike is that a number of them were built by only a few companies. One of the most prolific taxi body builders was Millspaugh & Irish Corporation of Indianapolis, Indiana. They would build and mount a taxi body on almost any chassis and even provided bodies for companies who could make their own, like Checker Cab Manufacturing of Kalamazoo, Michigan. Here was an example of their craft, a 1925 Dodge wearing a Millspaugh & Irish taxi body. *Manning Brothers*

RIGHT-HAND SIDE VIEW
OF THE BAUER
SHOWING FRONT DOOR AND
BAGGAGE CARRIER

BAUER CAB

Luggage Carrier for suit cases and small baggage folds flat on running board when not in use. A specially constructed strapping device attached to cowl accommodates steamer trunk. Takes up no room when not in use.

Page Six

One of the most unusual taxi designs of the 20th century had to be the 1926 Bauer Front Door Taxi Model B, built by the Bauer Taxicab Manufacturing Company at 2634-2636 South Michigan Avenue in Chicago. Its founder, Perry S. Bauer, felt that a taxi should have an entrance more like a house so he angled the rear passenger door inward to the point where the driver could reach over and open it. Bauer insisted that the left rear door was for emergencies only and it only had one handle on the outside where the operator could control it. Power was from a 22.5-hp Buda four-cylinder engine and the five-door taxi was priced out at $2,450, with the standard black and red paint job. Production numbers for Bauer's one year of production are unknown and it is thought that all of Bauer's output was used in Chicago only. *Henry Winningham*

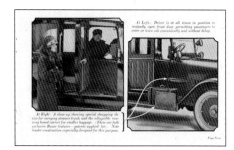

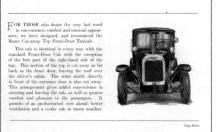

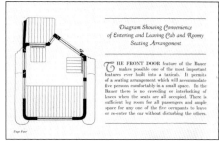

While it looked like a profound idea, the journey to the rear seat required a fare to bend over, go up some steps, turn to the left, and duck walk to the rear seat through the big door. *Henry Winningham*

As if the Bauer's layout wasn't interesting enough, they offered an option called the Cutaway Top that removed the right front roof so passengers wouldn't have to stoop under it to enter or exit. This left the driver with a skinny roof and a two-piece windshield. *Henry Winningham*

Bauer advertising explained that their design made it possible for five people to occupy a relatively small space with no crowding or interlocking of knees. Exiting without disturbing fellow passengers was also said to be possible although the folding jump seat in front of the main door looked problematic if occupied. The angled door could be left open in summer for ventilation and, from a profit standpoint, it also prevented anyone from leaving the cab unnoticed. *Henry Winningham*

This woman seemed pleased to be stepping out of a 1926 Hupmobile taxi into such a nice neighborhood. The Gotfredson Truck Company's Taxi Body Division in Detroit, Michigan, built the cab body. There was no right front door so luggage went next to the driver's bucket seat and the rear roof did not fold down despite the appearance of the landau bars. With jump seats, it had five-passenger capacity. Note the interesting, egg-shaped radiator ornament and the ornate, crowned availability lights mounted on the sides of the roof. The fare prices on the cowl were Manhattan rates. *Manning Brothers*

The interior of the Gotfredson Truck Company's Taxi Body Division showed the vast amount of woodwork that went into these custom taxi creations. *Manning Brothers*

A mid-1920s Pierce-Arrow Model 80 seven-passenger sedan did work as a taxi for a Century Cab Company. Powered by a 70-hp, six-cylinder motor, with the jump seats there was room for at least five in back. The dual sidemounts were not the kind of option you would find on a taxi so this cab was probably a lightly used luxury sedan in its first life. The passenger side spare is totally bald and worn down to the cord. *Nathan Willensky*

A 1926 GMC truck, with "Big Brute" painted on its front, hauled this nearly new Yellow as a display for the Yellow Cab Company of Los Angeles' celebration of 150 fresh taxis from the Yellow Cab Manufacturing Company of Chicago, Illinois. The sales slogans for the company centered around their low fares and the possibility that five passengers could ride for the price of one. *Nathan Willensky*

It took a police escort to get 150 Yellows in line for a photo in 1926. The previously shown GMC truck was seventh in line. *Nathan Willensky*

A proud, uniformed driver posed with his Los Angeles Yellow Cab, Number 101, in 1926. Mounted in the right front luggage area was a very large Ohmer meter that printed a receipt. Perhaps the driver wasn't aware or didn't care that Number 101 had bald tires. *Nathan Willensky*

The Five Boros cab was built by the M. P. Möller Motor Car Company of Hagertown, Maryland, for an operator in the New York City area. The name, Five Boros, referred to the five boroughs comprising the metropolitan area: Manhattan, Queens, Bronx, Brooklyn, and Staten Island. A stamped plate on the rear door was supposed to have a map showing the five boroughs. The license plates are New York State taxi plates since they begin with the letter "O." Both of these taxis had unusual chrome exhaust pipes and air vents coming out of their hoods but it is not known today if they were functional or not. Figures on how many were built and what years they operated are currently unknown but guesses are that the time period coincided with the M. P. Möller Company's factory built cab program which encompassed 1927 to 1931. *Nathan Willensky*

Cab Number 26 may have said "Checker Cab" on its rear doors but the taxi itself was a Yellow Cab Manufacturing product from the mid-1920s working for a Checker Cab Company. Number 26 experienced a side impact so abrupt that it caused both the driver and passenger to break their non-safety glass side windows. The front compartment had snap-on enclosures with built-in windows to make the taxi more livable in winter. *Henry Winningham*

The Paramount taxi was another M. P. Möller Motor Car Company creation and its life span was probably the same as the Five Boros: 1927 to 1931. Power was by a six-cylinder motor and its family resemblence to the preceeding Five Boros wasn't coincidental. Möller taxis frequently picked up the name of the taxi company that ordered them. For operators, it was classy to have a cab with your company name as the brand. This Paramount is wearing Manhattan rates not only on the cowl but also on a metal roof sign just behind the convertible top opening. Whether ordered in town car or sedan configuration, any Paramount taxi was impressive. *Oldee Taxi Instruments*

1927 Yellow Cab New York City.

New York City received 600 1927 Yellow Model 06 taxis like this one out of a total production of 2,598 units. As was typical for Manhattan, the cab was built without a right front door and the floor was given some ribs to minimize luggage movement. The outward appearance of the body was quite close to that of a Buick and even the engine was a Buick six-cylinder combined with a three-speed transmission. Headlights moved from the cowl to the front of the car this year and four-wheel brakes were standard for $2,450. The taxi medallion was on the cowl just below the rates. *Chris Monier*

Checker Cab Manufacturing came out with the attractive Model K in 1928 that not only was bigger and heavier than the old model but looked expensive, too. At $2,500 apiece, they were almost three times the cost of a base Plymouth or Ford taxi but buyers got a lot of cab for their money: Four-wheel hydraulic brakes, shatterproof glass, room for five in back, and a convertible roof over the driver were just some of the features found in the Model K. To move the grand cab around, a 61-hp Buda six-cylinder provided sedate motivation. This 1928 Model K belonged to Chicago Checker Cab and was photographed entering the shop garage, hopefully to get some new tires since all of them were bald. Even though it had landau irons, the rear roof did not fold down. The hand-operated spotlight on the left front windshield post no doubt came in handy for reading addresses at night. The round, checkerboard light on the building was a rather unique sentinel. *Henry Winningham*

Yellow Manufacturing sold 2,198 of these Model 06s in 1928 for a price of $2,150 each. Some of the cabs were built at the old Chicago factory and some were built at the new plant in Pontiac, Michigan. The Buick overhead valve six was still the Yellow's prime mover and Firestone tires were still standard. Open front town car taxis were available but numbers were modest and none have been seen in a long time. *Henry Winningham*

A row of five 1928 Yellow Model 06s served the Pontiac, Michigan, Yellow Cab Company and the drivers were all lined up in their spiffy uniforms. A child, sitting on a jump seat in the first cab, was peering out of the right front window. *Nathan Willensky*

Not every cab company was into town car taxis and Philadelphia, Pennsylvania's Mitten Transportation was one of them. They ordered 500 orange and black Model Ks with a full sedan roof that dispensed with the convertible top over the driver's seat and the faux landau bar treatment in the rear. When new, a series of adjustable louvers in front of the radiator were meant to maximize engine temperatures under winter conditions. To mark the different body type, this new model was known as the K2 and probably was available to anybody who wanted one. It is unknown today if any were used outside of Philadelphia. This photo was of a new K2 with "Quaker City Cabs, Inc., under Mitten Management" lettering on the rear doors. *Ben Merkel*

A 1931 insurance photo at Quaker City Cabs in Philadelphia revealed a Checker Model K2, Number 2133, wearing an original headlight lens on the passenger side and a Brand X on the right. Judging from the decent condition of this fairly new cab, it was probably being recorded for the slightly bent front bumper. The radiator had a crank hole near the bottom with a sliding cover to assist in low battery starts. The adjustable louvers in front of the radiator, present when the cab was new, have been removed. They might have become a pain to replace after several front end crashes. The tires were almost bald. Unfortunately, no K2 Checkers are known to be around today. *Nathan Willensky*

The reason Checkers used to cost three times as much as entry-level cabs is that they lasted at least three times as long. Mitten Transportation of Philadelphia was still hanging in there with the K2 fleet in 1935, as this insurance photo of a freshly damaged driver's door demonstrated. Old Number 2046 was wearing snow chains since they were normally required by law in many cities during snowfalls. The center roof light probably stayed on all the time and the colored sidelights were most likely availability or meter lights. Note how Number 2046's rear was hanging low, even when empty, compared to the previous photo of a new K2 where there was much more clearance between the rear tire and the fender. This was and is a common occurrence on all brands of taxis after hauling thousands of fares and their luggage. *Nathan Willensky*

The Ford Model A was a fairly popular cab with 4,900 being produced in 1928 and 1929 at a price of around $800 each. For this money, the operator got a front bucket seat trimmed in imitation leather, an offset partition, room for three passengers on the velour rear seat, and a single rear-facing jump seat that folded into the divider. The body style was referred to as the 135-A. Mechanically, a truck clutch became standard equipment in October 1929 and the rear axle ratio was raised to 9:37 for city use. This 1929 Model A was in service with the General Cab Company of Oregon and, judging from the driver's uniform and tall boots, either General Cab was trying to upscale their Ford taxi rides or the outfits were required by law. The taxicab body, by itself, could be purchased new from Ford for $465 F.O.B. Detroit. *Nathan Willensky*

1929 was Yellow Manufacturing's last year before it became General and 1,888 units were built with prices staying at $2,150. This Model 06 was used in Oregon as Yellow Cab Number 70, probably in a big city like Portland, and featured heavy-duty wheel hubs with "GMC" on the chrome caps. Styling differences from 1928 were minor and included less space between the doors, bigger bumpers, new radiator, and headlights. The oval taxi light was rather novel. A spotlight was standard equipment. *Nathan Willensky*

Yellow Manufacturing's top offering in 1929 was the swan song for its town car cabs. The interior of this new Model 06 displayed the "V" shaped windshield, snap-on convertible top, and front doors with no upper frames that made these taxis so special. It is unknown how many open cabs were built this year but chances are that it wasn't many. A chrome vertical taxi sign was attached to the right front windshield post and the lettering was put on at the factory in Pontiac, Michigan. To top off this elegant Yellow, the front fenders were designed for side-mounted spare tires. With all the extras, a Model 06 town car was one of a select few that could give Checker's Model K a run for its money. *Nathan Willensky*

1930 to 1954

The Depression and World War II were not easy years for the taxi industry but this time period did produce some very interesting for-hire vehicles. When the stock market crashed in 1929, and thousands of Americans were thrown out of work, they no longer had money for taxi rides. What had once been a growing industry slowed to a crawl and ultimately turned into a free-for-all as desperate operators slashed their rates to stay competitive. In some circumstances, they were doing battle not only with each other but also against local streetcar companies and it proved a nightmare for all parties concerned. The public, even though they may have had fairly low rates, paid for it in other ways. Not surprisingly, riders were routinely subject to overcharging, brusque behavior regarding tip amounts, lack of compensation after accidents, and poor equipment condition brought on by endless deferred maintenance. They were also befuddled by inconsistent taxi rates and signage, the dizzying array of cars calling themselves taxis, and nobody was really sure who was behind the wheels of some of these cabs. The years spent during the 1920s making the taxi driver out to be the well-dressed gentleman were undone.

To tame the taxi tiger, regulations began to surface, not only in the public's interest, but those borne of struggling fleet operators searching for a level playing field. Proposals in many cities involved placing taxicabs under control of the state, city utility commission, or even the police department. The number of licenses, or medallions, to operate a taxi within a certain metropolitan area was to be limited and regulated. For example, in 1930, Boston froze the number of licensed cabs at 1,525, in 1934, Chicago's number was 4,108, and three years later New York froze the number of hacks at 13,500. Some of these numbers would fluctuate over the years but the idea spread and most US cities have had a limit on the number of licensed operating taxis for a long time. These numbers are frequently based on an area's ideal population-to-cab ratio, a figure that is supposed to provide decent service for the public while giving the cab operator enough business to support their family. Other remedies for a sick industry were routinely inspected meters, fixed rates, taxi age limitations, and periodic vehicle inspections, all of which are still in use today.

New York City went one step further and enacted a daunting set of regulations that effectively locked almost every make of taxi out of the city until 1954 by requiring four-door vehicles with five-passenger capacities in the rear, which usually meant a long wheelbase sedan with jump seats. The driver had to have a bucket seat in order to preclude passengers up front and a privacy partition was needed to seperate the drivers from their fares. To prevent nefarious Prohibition uses, taxis had to have a baffle in the trunk so it couldn't be used and a bumper-mounted trunk rack replaced this space

The 1930 Studebaker Model 53, which a few months earlier had been known as the Erskine Model 53, was a decent cab for $965, out the door with the 205-ci flathead six and a three-speed stick on the floor. Even though Studebaker was locked out of big markets like New York City and Chicago, it was quite content to sell a ton of cabs to rural towns and cities where low cost was king. Unlike its big city counterparts, this Model 53 had no partition, a full bench seat in front, and room for three adults in the rear. Since there's a spare tire and no trunk, where the luggage went is another small town mystery. Note the "Hertz Drivurself" signs all over the Yellow Cab building. Hertz's Yellow Drive-it-Yourself was a program, started in 1924, which rented modified taxis to the public. *Nathan Willensky*

so law enforcement could plainly see what was being transported. New York City was one of seven cities requiring a specialty vehicle by 1932. Only Checker Cab Manufacturing, Chrysler, General Motors, and, later on, Packard, had assembly line models which either met these requirements or could be adapted to pass. In terms of overall volume, only 15% of the 17,000 cabs on the road in the U.S. at this time were purpose-built units. Then, as now, The Hack Bureau allowed periodic, small fleets to operate on an experimental basis and this resulted in some interesting-but-obscure mini fleets. Whether they were custom bodied taxis, foreign taxis, station wagon cabs, or alternative fuel vehicles, this metropolis has certainly considered a wide variety of vehicles over the years, although few experimental taxis ever seem to result in large fleet buys. New York City isn't alone in trying new taxi concepts but being such a large taxi market it is frequently a bellwether for other towns.

Outside of the big cities, small town operators weren't subject to much regulation at all and, much like today, they were more than content to either purchase late model used taxis from a big city fleet or secure lightly used private cars and make them into cabs. For those with the money, practically every brand of new four-door sedan built in America had options like heavy-duty clutch, upgraded springs, and larger radiator, which made them taxi contestants. Most cars could handle serenely cruising Main Street, USA, delivering passengers, packages, and supplies to shut-ins on a part-time basis. Unlike their big city counterparts, many small cab companies thought nothing of operating 12-year-old equipment, and many still don't. In rural areas, brands with the cheapest and easiest-to-get parts usually dominated and that normally meant Chevrolet, Pontiac, Oakland, Plymouth, Dodge, DeSoto, Studebaker, and Ford, just to name a few. Checker, despite being a major big city heavyweight, also played some small towns. But to get spare parts frequently meant calling up one of Checker's big parts depots and having items shipped-a negative sometimes when a cab was down.

With the old fabric roofs being replaced by steel, it was now easier for taxi operators to affix lighted roof domes and this predictably ended the reign of the vertical, illuminated sign attached to the windshield post. Cab-mounted advertising signs were still in their infancy and few prewar cabs carried any ads at all. Some may have placed round ads on their rear-mounted spare tires and few may have had bumper stickers from some restaurant. For the most part they were ad devoid until the 1950s. Inside taxis, the huge, floor mounted, pedestal meters slimmed down enough to fit in the dashboard or even a glovebox by the late 1940s. The for-hire industry's utilization of the two-way radio during World War II proved to be such a boon to productivity that it became a virtual necessity for anybody wanting to make a go of it in the taxi business. The old-fashioned taxi call box became a quaint relic.

Since Checker Cab Manufacturing owned Cleveland, Ohio's Yellow Cab Company for a time, it made sense that they used their own products, as evidenced by this unusual Checker Model K posing in a lush suburb. Number 330's rear compartment had no center posts and whether the windows came up and made a seal like today's hardtops or if there were posts that the driver had to take out is unknown today. The cab must have been pretty special, as it wore a hood from the next year's model, and the louvers were chromed. A spotlight and windshield-mounted vertical chrome "Yellow" sign gave this remarkable taxi a very rich appearance. A pouch for the snap-on top was suspended behind the driver's head. When Checker sold Cleveland Yellow Cab to a local entrepreneur in 1934, a switch was made to Plymouth automobiles and the old Checkers like this one faded quickly. The average life of a cab in Cleveland at this time was 300,000 miles but, by the late 1950s, it had dropped to 150,000 because the huge surge in private automobiles had relaxed the demand for taxis. Currently, cabs in Cleveland can rack up 350,000 miles within their legal five-year lifetime without much trouble. *Ben Merkel*

For cab drivers, the evolution of the taxi during the 1930s brought an end to their choice of blue skies or not as the open-front town car taxicabs quietly disappeared by the end of the decade. While these grand machines were extremely impressive, by 1935 they were from another era as streamlined, new cars with stamped steel bodies weren't as easy to modify as the old wood framed ones. This formal body style would live on in high-end cars but, for taxi drivers, the party was over. The passenger's party, however, was just getting started with the introduction of the rear sunroof on some 1935 Checkers and DeSotos. GM's General taxi came in with their sliding sunroof option the following year. Cars advanced so fast in terms of design and style that a 1936 DeSoto made its 1930 predecessor look archaic. For all brands, power was up under the hood and synchronized transmissions replaced the non-synchronized, "crashbox" units, which required a lot of double-clutching to avoid gear clashing. One of the few negatives for drivers was the moving of the stick shift transmission from the floor to the steering column by car manufacturers in the late 1930s. While fine when new, these "three-on-the-tree" shifters would get sloppy after high use and tended to block shifts or send the unfortunate driver into a gearless limbo.

While he may have had lots of armoured limousines at his disposal, mobster Al Capone and his legal team regularly took cabs to Chicago Federal Courthouse appearances. Here Capone is exiting a Checker Model K from the Chicago Yellow Cab Company on October 10, 1931. It is said that payment to the driver was normally handled through one of Mr. Capone's ubiquitous bodyguards. In this view, the snap-on nature of the convertible roof over the driver's seat is evident. The vertical, chromed box attached to the right windshield post is a taxi sign with "Yellow" spelled out in illuminated, block letters. *New York Daily News/Henry Winningham*

In 1939, Checker Cab Manufacturing decided to give its competitors a heart attack with its radical Model A taxi featuring a steel, clamshell roof over the rear seat that would electrically pivot into the trunk area with the touch of a button. On those days when a lowered top was inappropriate, a sunroof known as the Air-N-Lite, was also available in addition to the open rear area. Checker didn't forget the driver either since an optional, roof-mounted air vent over the front seat provided some heat relief in the days before air-conditioned taxis. Even though the Model A was only in production for two years, many of them served during the war and left a strong impression on those passengers lucky enough to ride in them with the top down. For taxi riders, this open-air experience in cities like New York City and Chicago must have been heady stuff and has to qualify as one of the last great American taxi passenger experiences of the 20th century. It is also remarkable that it took one of the smallest domestic automakers, Checker Cab Manufacturing, to design and build a taxi so over-the-top that it gave its

big Detroit competition nowhere to go. Unfortunately for riders, a German fellow named Adolf Hitler caused Model A production to end in 1941.

America's entry into World War II was a nightmare for taxi operators, as they could no longer buy new equipment after 1942. For fleets used to getting new cabs every year or two, they now had to keep their current taxis running indefinitely. The rationing of gasoline and endless recapping of worn tires was compounded by a chronic shortage of spare parts that kept broken taxis off the road with no replacements. In cities with special, long wheelbase taxis, some operators couldn't substitute a three-in-the-rear stock sedan in place of a totalled five-in-the-rear limousine bodied cab so they were particularly hard pressed to keep equipment on the streets. To complete the misery index, ridership went up while the supply of taxis went down because many factories and military bases were humming 24 hours a day and people needed to get to them. To be as efficient as possible, many taxis were packed with riders. To make sure everybody behaved, the Office of Defense Transportation in 1942 implemented some wartime rules such as no taxi cruising, no recreational trips, no goods deliveries, no speeding, no trips more than 10 miles outside city limits, and no trips longer than 35 miles. Taxicabs were given an S-type fuel-rationing card, which allowed them a maximum of about 100 miles per day.

By 1945, most of the taxis in the US were a mess. By estimates of the time, it was figured that about a quarter of the nation's taxis were in the shop on any given day. More than a few of the prewar taxis went over a half million miles and the accompanying repair costs were so high that they almost equalled the cost of a new cab before the war. In Chicago, once the new 1946 taxis came out, the clapped-out, prewar Checkers were offered to the public at $10 for non-runners and $15 for runners. Due to their condition, however, there were few takers and most were scrapped. Operators were so desperate for new cars that some opted for brands they didn't normally use until supply caught up with demand in the late 1940s. Missing from the lineup of new, postwar taxis was any hint of a convertible top from any US cab maker. DeSoto Skyviews still had a sunroof option but it only lasted from 1946 to 1948. For taxi riders, they had been to the top of the mountain with elaborate landaulets and sliding glass sunroofs but now things were going downhill. The last vestiges of old-fashioned taxi gentility, like cavernous interiors and folding jump seats, were found at just two manufacturing companies by 1951: Checker and Chrysler. With the pickings getting slim, it was no surprise that most cities had backed down from their prewar dictums regarding specialized vehicles such as cabs. New York City, long in love with their beloved jumbo taxis, was the last to let them go in 1954.

DeSoto and Plymouth were almost identical this year and shared the same base motor, a four-cylinder flathead. New to the cab game, DeSoto would catch up fast. This was a 1930 DeSoto taxi, probably a Model K, working in San Francisco, California. The light on the passenger side of the sun visor over the windshield looks like an availability light to let people know if the cab was engaged or not. *San Francisco Public Library*

A 1931 Chevrolet Special sedan worked for a currently unknown Yellow Cab Company as Number 157. While the trunk rack was a normal addition to a taxicab, the side-mounted spare tires were not since decent, exposed spare tires had a bad habit of disappearing, so some fleet taxis either didn't carry a spare or they had a baldie suitable for a quick run to the shop and no further. The radiator's optional quail mascot was another unlikely taxi option so this could well have been a private car that was made into a cab. 50-hp six-cylinder motors displacing 194 cubic inches powered Chevrolets. *Nathan Willensky*

One of Checker Manufacturing's most dramatic cabs came out this year for a two season run: the Model M. Powered by a Buda six-cylinder engine, these taxis were offered in two wheelbases, a regular six window sedan or a long model for train station runs. With the acquisition of Parmelee Transportation in late 1929, Checker took control of about 7,500 cars, trucks, and buses used to ferry railroad passengers and freight between terminals. This restored Model M is the only known survivor in roadworthy condition. *Joe Fay*

Chicago Checker Cab, since it had been buying Checkers pretty much since birth, was used to the idea of buying new cabs from themselves, but for Chicago Yellow Cab it was a new experience to order from Kalamazoo and not Chicago. Until John Hertz relinquished final control of Chicago Yellow Cab in 1929, the cab company had been buying from General Motors' Yellow Manufacturing Division. Now, in a twist of irony, a 1931 or 1932 Checker Model M poses in front of Chicago's Drake Hotel wearing Yellow Cab markings. *Henry Winningham*

This new 1931 General Model 0-12 was one of 150 built for the Palace Cab Company of New York City. Note the interesting arrow-shaped turn signals on the front fenders. A spotlight and horn were standard equipment as was a trap door in the floor that allowed for meter transmission inspections. These popular cabs rode on a 122-inch wheelbase and were powered by a 257-ci, six-cylinder GMC motor and a three-speed manual transmission. Jump seats allowed for 5-in-the-rear seating behind the partition and the driver sat on a black leather bucket seat with the customer's luggage. Rear upholstery was available in mohair or leather. The meter in this cab was an Ohmer. *Detroit Public Library*

Ads touted that the General taxi bodies used only the finest seasoned lumber and that the running boards were made of 10-gauge steel to last. Like other taxi manufacturers, General would alter a body style or paint a cab any color or combination of colors to make a sale. Approximately 1,813 Generals came out of the Pontiac, Michigan, truck plant in 1931. *Henry Winningham*

Checker brought out their new Model T in 1933 and built it until late 1934. The cars were mildly restyled but a Lycoming straight eight motor replaced the Buda six and operators soon found that the new eight got better gas mileage probably because the bigger engines were less stressed. This particular cab was part of the Checker-owned Parmelee System in New York City and wore its taxi medallion on the lower right portion of the cowl. These were the last town car style cabs that Checker would build. *Nathan Willensky*

This 1933 General Model 0-14 was destined for Des Moines, Iowa, Yellow Cab. Unlike Checker, General didn't offer a town car body style and concentrated instead on their seven-passenger sedan line. The General Cab was a custom built, slightly stretched, stock Fisher body mounted on a light truck chassis. A Chevrolet -Pontiac sedan body was lengthened and cutting two regular doors and welding the long sections together created the rear doors. When most Chevrolet sedans had wire wheels, the Generals had commercial, steel rims with small, "bottlecap" hubcaps that read "General." Estimates put this year's General production at 2,423 in 1933 and only 96 in 1934. General didn't make a car in 1935. At least one restored 1933 General is still around. *Nathan Willensky*

While the General Cab Division took 1935 off, regular GM sedan taxis sold well outside of major cities where there were no rules regarding specialized cabs. In rural America, Chevrolet and Pontiac taxis were very popular since they provided good service for a relatively low cost. Regular features on the 1936 Pontiac taxi package were a partition with a folding jump seat, heavy-duty clutch, radiator, and wheel rims. The lights on the roof were availability lights that came on and off with the meter and let people on the street know whether a cab was engaged or not. *Nathan Willensky*

A pair of Checker Model Ys lined up in front of the famous French liner, *Normandie*, probably near the French Line's Pier in New York City. The front cab was a Parmelee Transportation unit and had an optional glass skylight in the rear with the words "Air-N-Lite Glass Top" along the side of the roof edge. The *Normandie* was launched amidst much fanfare in 1935 but only served six years before being seized by the US government in 1941. Efforts to convert it into a troopship failed when fire broke out and excess water caused the ship to sink at the pier early in 1942. *Corbis*

The Los Angeles Yellow Cab Company employed a large fleet of 1935 Airstream taxis as evidenced by this major lineup in front of the cab company. Strangely, while the fleet looks similar to the Airstream shown previously, the front bumpers on these Los Angleles cabs are not curved. Whether the cab company or Chrysler changed them, beefing up existing bumper systems was, and still is, a time honored taxi tradition. Los Angeles Yellow Cab Company would try Buick taxis before the decade was out. *DaimlerChrysler*

The DeSoto Airstream was a very competent taxi and developed a loyal following from coast to coast. Like its competitors, a bucket seat and partition were regular options so luggage or packages could ride up front when no trunk was specified. It is highly probable that a trunk-back sedan was also available with the taxi package. The taxi roof light was modern for its day and the conical sidelights over the rear doors were meter lights. An L head six-cylinder engine that boasted 93 horsepower coupled to a three-speed transmission powered the 3,000-lb sedan. The Airstream's larger sibling, the Airflow, saw limited use as a taxicab. *DaimlerChrysler*

The Checker Model Y was built from 1935 to 1939 and all are thought to have had a 148 horsepower Lycoming eight with a three speed floor shift. Cabbies liked Checker's peppy new motor and were most pleased to find that it gave better fuel economy than the six before it. This Model Y Yellow Cab was in stock form and had no air vent or glass sunroof. The driver got a leather, bucket seat next to a crank-up, glass partition. *Nathan Willensky*

For the first time in a long time, Checker Cab Manufacturing didn't have a town car in their lineup. One reason for its demise was that few cabbies drove with the convertible top open. Checker's solution was the new, 1935 Model Y with an optional air vent over the driver and an extra cost, glass sunroof, called the Air-N-Lite, in the rear. This restored 1936 example, wearing Parmelee System decals, sports both of those options. Only two Model Ys are known to exist today- this one is owned by Checker Motors and resides at the Gilmore Museum in Hickory Corners, Michigan and one unrestored example, that had been cut down into a tow truck by a cab company, is awaiting restoration out West. *Gilmore Museum*

A large number of Checker Model Ys sit dormant during a general strike at the Brooklyn garage of Parmelee Transportation in 1939. A total of 7,000 cabs were idled after drivers were called out by the Transport Workers Union in support of demands for a larger share of receipts. Checker Cab Manufacturing owned Parmelee Transportation. All the cabs pictured have glass sunroofs in the rear. *Nathan Willensky*

A group of old and new taxis mixed at a hot spot in the mid 1930s, probably at a pier in New York City. The Checker Model Y in the lower left was a green, beige, and white Bell Cab and behind it and to the right rear were two Checker Model Ms from the Parmelee System. From this viewpoint, the Model M's interesting hood and cowl paint treatment can be seen. Note how the checkerboard decals dwindle down along with the dark paintwork as the center of the hood is reached. *Henry Winningham*

With General Motors, Chrysler, and Checker out of the town car cab business, the Town Taxi Company of New York City took matters into their own hands by having the M. P. Möller Motor Car Company of Hagerstown, Maryland, build them some stylish, five-passenger town car cab bodies mounted on the new 1936 Diamond T light duty truck chassis for use in the Manhattan area only. These might be the last taxis with the town car style convertible top over the driver's seat. The roof light resembled a series of five buildings with the center one being the tallest. A domed, amber light topped off each building. Since the taxi's cowl was so short, the New York City taxi medallion just barely squeezed into the space between the front door and the hood. It is unknown how many of these remarkable cabs were constructed in 1936 and 1937 and none have surfaced in recent times. *Henry Winningham*

A policeman on horseback was funneling traffic around this lineup of new 1936 Chevrolet taxis for the Checker Cab Company of Detroit, Michigan. For those not needing a five-in-the-rear capability, the regular wheelbase Chevrolets made sense and GM could price them right since they didn't require special bodywork and inexpensive parts were available at any Chevy dealer. Detroit Checker Cab Company, like most fleets, tended to buy cars based on which car dealer could give them the best price for a large number of units. In 1937, for example, Detroit Checker Cab bought some Plymouths. *Detroit Public Library*

DeSoto had come a long way since 1930. The 1936 DeSoto Custom long wheelbase taxi was a strong player on the East and West Coasts. It is estimated that 2,951 taxis were built in 1936. *Peter Kanze*

This 1936 DeSoto S-1 Sunshine taxi from New York City was wearing New York State Fair taxi plates. The center mounted bumper guard was installed at the factory and no doubt earned its keep in heavy traffic. The roof sign read "Sunshine Radio," which referred to a meter-activated music radio in the rear for customers. This cab was missing its windshield wipers. *Nathan Willensky*

To meet the five-in-the-rear laws of places like New York City, DeSoto reached into its lineup and commercialized their seven-passenger S-1 Airstream trunkless sedan for taxi service by installing a partition, a front bucket seat, and heavy-duty floor mats. This way, they didn't have to custom craft a special body just for the taxi market. The stamped tinplate on the rear door was a Sunshine logo. *Peter Kanze*

With the rear door open, the leather seat beckons for us to come closer. On a nice day in Manhattan with the sunroof open, cab rides must have been pretty agreeable to passengers. *Peter Kanze*

With the sunroof open on a nice day, it was easy to get a little crazy as these passengers on Fifth Avenue were showing. On this Sunshine cab, even the driver got a glass window over his head. *Henry Winningham*

A peek at the rear of this DeSoto reveals the obligatory trunk rack for New York City complete with a leather belt for making trunks stay put. Virtually all taxis with trunk racks had to have at least one belt. With turn signals not commonplace on cars yet, this cab had just one light in the rear consisting of a combination stop and cruise light. "Downtown" also insisted that taxi license plates in Manhattan be mounted way up on top of the trunklid where they would always be viewable. In most cab manufacturer's parts books of this era, New York City usually had its own special rear license plate holders. *Peter Kanze*

1936 DeSoto-NYC Sunshine- Advertising for Sunshine Cab. *Henry Winningham*

A Swift, Safe, Sleek

"SUNSHINE" TAXI

Will Take You to and from the Theatre (or Any Other Place) in Grand Style and at Very Small Cost!

•

For a Smooth, Pleasant Ride—

HAIL A

"SUNSHINE" CAB

When You Leave the Theater or Telephone CIrcle 7-2323

•

Special Rates for Pre-arranged Theater Parties

This 1936 DeSoto smashup at 19th Street and 7th Avenue in Manhattan resulted in a leg injury for its sole passenger, a woman named Alexandria Ladner. In the days before seat belts and airbags, even a low speed collision like this one could send you to the hospital. Note how the impact made the windshield open and caused the center sunburst on the roof sign to fly off. *Nathan Willensky*

Only a few 1936 DeSoto Sunshine cabs exist today and most of them survived because movie studio prop departments kept a large number of old taxis until the early 1970s. Here is a restored DeSoto S-1 Sunshine at Harrah's Auto Museum in Nevada. *Henry Winningham*

Pontiac continued to sell its six-cylinder sedans to the taxi trade and San Diego was the recipient of this pretty Black and White cab. Ordered in the slantback version without a trunk, luggage went up front next to the driver's bucket seat. This cab had three-in-the-rear capability unless the partition had a flip down jump seat, which would have raised its capacity by at least one. Normal taxi options included a larger radiator, clutch, and beefed up springs. To keep their cabs from looking too much like police cars, checkerboard decals were commonly used to set them apart. Pontiac sold these taxis for under $800. *Chris Monier*

This stunning General Model 0-16 Black and White Cab highlighted the myriad of paint patterns available to the taxi purchaser. If a fleet owner wanted their new cars painted a certain way, it was not unusual for a manufacturer to send out a black and white outline for the ordering person to fill in with colors. This new paint pattern would normally be kept at the factory in case the client came back for seconds. Judging from the attractive way the window frames and wheel rims were ordered in white, it suggests that the Black and White Cab Company spent some time thinking about visual impact. *Nathan Willensky*

For St. Paul, Minnesota, Blue and White Cab, their General Model 0-16 seemed to be heavy in blue and light on white. Under the hood, all Generals had the proven 206.8-ci, valve-in-head six cylinder coupled to a floor mounted three-speed transmission with synchromesh on second and third speeds. The roof was all steel and General promoted it as the "Turret-Top." *Nathan Willensky*

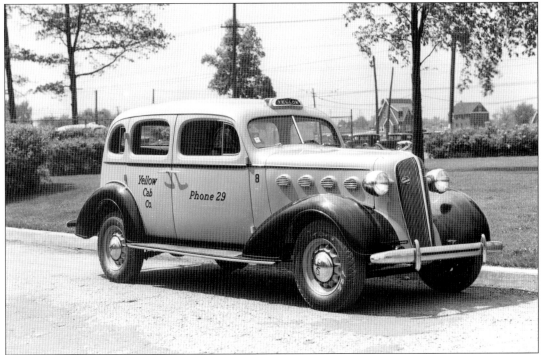

The Yellow Cab Company in Fairmount, West Virginia, spent a little more and bought GM's finest taxi in 1936. Approximately 3,500 Generals came out of the Pontiac, Michigan factory at a cost of $965 F.O.B. each. If a buyer wanted it, these big cabs could be ordered with Chevrolet or Pontiac nameplates. *Nathan Willensky*

The Model 0-16 interior was roomy and modern. Available in leather or mohair, there was room for five behind the partition but it could probably have turned into a very cozy six, if need be. The partition was advertised as being easy to remove in the event an owner wanted to turn the cab into a regular sedan with a full front seat. *Ben Merkel*

A 1936 General driver's compartment came with a black, adjustable leather bucket seat and partition or a full bench seat without it. The Model 0-16 sedan with a full front seat allowed for at least eight passenger capacity and was promoted as a good crew vehicle, family car, or undertaker's limousine. *Ben Merkel*

It was no secret that taxi manufacturers would go the extra mile to make a customer choose their brand and GM was no exception. If somebody wanted to buy 100 cabs, that equalled a hunk of change even with the fleet discount. This unusual 1936 General Model 0-16 was destined for the Tulsa Cab Company in Tulsa, Oklahoma, and it featured a hinged sunroof over the rear seating area. Fisher Body most likely put it there but that information has not been confirmed. Some optional sliding sunroofs, which were very much like DeSoto's, were seen on some Generals in New York City belonging to the Allied System. *Nathan Willensky*

A yard full of decommissioned 1936 General 0-16s await disposal in Boston during the late 1940s. Once proud representatives of Boston's Checker Cab Company, a couple of hard-working years and World War II service had reduced them to rubble. Currently, no roadworthy 1936 Generals are known to exist although a 1937 example remains. *Nathan Willensky*

Chrysler had a full line of seven-passenger sedans and they weren't afraid to sell them as cabs under the Plymouth, DeSoto, or Dodge banners. With a major class wheelbase of 132 inches, this big Plymouth had front and rear doors substantially longer than those found on the stock six-passenger sedans. This particular cab did service in San Diego, California, and even though it had a trunk, it was ordered with the front bucket seat and partition so luggage could go up front. The round lights on the side of the roof would normally come on to let potential customers know whether a cab was available or not. *Henry Winningham*

Sadly, 1938 was the last year for the long wheelbase General Motors Cab. While the long bodies would live on a little longer as export limousines, their taxi face would disappear. This very attractive General Model 0-18 was likely headed for New York City, and Fisher Body sent it off with all the toys: Trunk rack, partition with leather bucket seat, two-tone paint job, and even a sliding sunroof. Base price for the fastback version was $1,076 and the trunkback version was $1,102. None of these 1938s have surfaced recently. *Nathan Willensky*

Toye Brothers Yellow Cab in New Orleans, Louisiana, ordered up some of the last Generals in 1938. After a mediocre year in 1937, with around 442 coming out of the GM truck plant, 1938 was even worse with only 387. For all the work required to build these specialized cabs, from splicing bodies and fabricating doors, it wasn't working out. This General Model 0-18 had the optional Chevrolet nameplates. Toye Brothers had been in the transportation business since 1852 and they liked to promote that their Yellow Cabs were instantly available at all hotels, train stations, and 50 convenient sub-stations around the New Orleans area and that all of their cabs had a privacy partition. *Nathan Willensky*

Considering its ownership by Checker Cab Manufacturing since 1929, Chicago Yellow bought Checkers nearly all the time and this 1939 to 1941 Model A was photographed with some enthusiastic fares in the back seat. Under the hood, the Lycoming eight had been replaced by a 262-ci Continental six-cylinder flathead similar to those used in some Brockway and Divco light-duty trucks. Chicago Yellow and Checker both ordered their Model A taxis with the optional Air-N-Lite sunroofs. *Henry Winningham*

The Model A interior was ultra modern and well appointed. Even the inside of the disappearing top was upholstered. Lower door panels were washable plastic. *Henry Winningham*

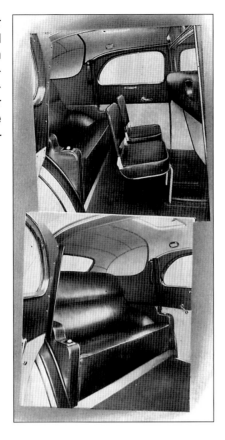

New York City had a heavy Checker presence for the same reason Chicago did: Checker Cab Manufacturing owned some major fleets in town. This 1939 to 1941 Checker Model A was caught reposing with its top up on a cold day in New York. The Automat in the background was once a popular fast food chain in the Manhattan area where vending machines dispensed sandwiches and beverages to patrons with change supplied by an attendant. While there used to be many of them, the last one closed in the mid 1990s. *Nathan Willensky*

Since General Motors and Chrysler had joined Checker in the rear sunroof arena, it was time for tiny Checker to give the big boys a heart attack and it did so in 1939 with its Model A. For lucky passengers in the furthest seat, the entire rear steel roof pivoted electrically into the body providing a true convertible experience although the roof seam was known to drip in heavy rain. When the weather was poor and the rear roof was closed, an optional glass sunroof in the center of the roof still allowed a view up. Checker called this the Air-N-Lite. The driver wasn't forgotten. An adjustable air scoop built into the front roof for the days before air conditioning could be ordered. *Henry Winningham*

The new Checker Model A dash was a simple, funtional affair with full instrumentation and adjustable driver's seat with at least 15 different positions. The floor-mounted stick shift had moved up to the steering column and Checker ads touted that it was not only easier to shift up there but that it freed up valuable luggage space to the right of the driver's bucket seat. *Henry Winningham*

When the top went down on a Checker Model A, it tended to put people in a good mood, as these two ladies demonstrated in the back of a brand new Chicago Yellow Cab parked quixotically in a theater lobby. The rear combination stop and cruise light had "Yellow" spelled out on the red lens where "Checker" usually was. *Henry Winningham*

From this angle, the optional air scoop over the driver is clearly seen. Note the flame-shaped availability lights on the side of the roof. *Henry Winningham*

After World War II, most taxi fleets were clamoring for new equipment and, as the new cabs slowly trickled in, all brands of prewar cabs suddenly became so-much-a-pound scrap or you could buy one to drive away for $15 to $30. After five long years of being nursed well past their prime, these Checkers from Pittsburg Yellow Cabs were spent. The hand-operated spotlights mounted at the top of the left front roof post were a Pittsburg Yellow trademark for years and graced their Checkers until the last ones were retired around 1988. *Nathan Willensky*

In 1943, this Checker Model A belonging to the Chicago Checker Cab Company was allegedly stolen by two drunken sailors trying to get back to the Navy pier. The pair got disoriented and almost drove the taxi into Lake Michigan. Note how the rear roof opened slightly from the impact with the breakwater. Only one Model A Checker is known to exist today. *Henry Winningham*

While cab driving is always rated near the top in dangerous occupations, during a cold Ohio winter in 1940 it was the passenger who was killed in this Cleveland Yellow Cab. The rear passenger vent window of this 1939 Plymouth Roadking taxi had been shattered by a bullet hole and the Cleveland police were on the scene. The man standing by the right front fender was Eliot Ness, Cleveland's Safety Director from 1935 to 1942. Ness previously achieved fame in Chicago as the government agent who was credited with helping to bring down gangster Al Capone. He earned the nickname "Untouchable," since he wouldn't take a bribe. In 1939, Plymouth built taxis in two wheelbases, the regular 114-inch version shown here, or the rare 134-inch, seven-passenger version. The paint scheme is interesting as are the three somewhat crooked availability lights mounted on the front of the roof. *Ben Merkel*

While Buick was known as a prestige automobile, it had a little sideline selling beefed-up four-door sedans to cab companies like Los Angeles Yellow Cab. While being a tad pricey to purchase and maintain, a former garage worker reported that the 1939 Buicks gave good service and clocked 500,000 miles before retirement. The familiar, time-tested, straight eight Buick engine worked a three-speed manual transmission with a heavy-duty clutch. A larger generator and bigger brake linings helped give this upscale car some taxi street credentials. Each of these Buicks had a bucket seat and partition. The cabs in the center were missing their rear tires so the intention must have been for all the Buicks to stay put. The triangular roof light was a rather arresting design. *Nathan Willensky*

Buick taxis were offered with a partition that curved around the driver and allowed enough room for a two person, folding jump seat that faced rearwards. While it must have been a pretty chummy set-up when fully loaded, it did give the Buick driver that option of making more money in areas where operators could charge for each person in the cab. Some optional bumper guards were tubular steel with a large, single guard in the middle made by an aftermarket supplier like Budd Bar Inc. *Henry Winningham*

Buick's new Underseat Heater supplies warm air both front and rear and allows use of defroster and fresh air intake tube which takes in fresh air at driver's breathing level.

Tubular bumpers as shown or rod type as shown on large center spread picture are available, giving added protection to front grille and rear trunk.

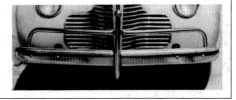

Out of General Motor's car divisions, it seemed like only Cadillac was staying away from yellow paint jobs. In 1940, Buick was hustling right along with Chevrolet and Pontiac for a piece of that taxi pie but they only promoted regular wheelbase four-door sedans and not stripped-down versions of their premium, eight-passenger Limited bodies. Buick probably took one look at the results of the now-defunct General Cab and decided not to join the battle between DeSoto and Checker. *Nathan Willensky*

Packard, like Buick, was a prestige brand that wasn't afraid to be seen working city streets at 3 a.m. Dealers had been selling cars for years with optional heavy-duty components but the push for taxi sales at Packard seemed to pick up steam beginning around 1940 and continued for almost 10 years. To handle taxi sales, Packard opened up Federal Packard Corporation at 1775 Broadway in New York City. Federal operated outside of the normal dealer network. Judging from the license plates and 25 cent fare on the front doors of these 1940 Packard City Cabs, they were probably going to Baltimore, Maryland. *Nathan Willensky*

During the war years, some requirements like metal taxi medallions and front license plates were waived to help the wartime scrap drives. *Nathan Willensky*

The long wheelbase DeSotos became Skyviews in 1940 instead of Sunshine Cabs. Current belief is that all of the long wheelbase DeSoto taxis sold from the James F. Waters DeSoto-Plymouth dealerships in Long Island City, New York and San Francisco, California, were considered Skyviews even if they didn't state it. Briggs Manufacturing of Detroit would send the painted bodies without glass to the Waters plant in Detroit for final outfitting. *Nathan Willensky*

While this 1940 DeSoto Skyview and the S. Klein-on-the-Square Annex Clothing Store in the backround are long gone, this is what the area next to Union Square in Manhattan used to look like in the early 1940s. The DeSoto wore a large, comprehensive bumper guard and was showing off one of the Skyview roof lights. The top part of the sign read "DeSoto" and the larger, lower half read "Skyview." The four globes around the sign were decorative. The taxi medallion was still found on the lower cowl. Under the hood, all large DeSotos were powered by a six-cylinder flathead motor putting out 105 horsepower. About 2,323 DeSoto Skyviews were constructed this year, almost double the number of civilian seven-passenger bodies built. *Nathan Willensky*

Boston had big DeSotos just like Manhattan. A 1940 DeSoto Skyview working for Boston Checker Cab posed for an insurance photo after it had been hit in the rear. *Chris Monier*

Outside of the major cities, DeSoto sold plenty of regular wheelbase taxis to smaller towns where they not only served as passenger conveyences but as mail and cargo haulers as well. A 1941 DeSoto, belonging to Gainer's Cab in Elkins, West Virginia, hooked up with an American Airlines DC-3 for a postal exchange right next to the runway. For rural America in the 1940s, this was the fastest way to send anything. *Nathan Willensky*

James Waters and his DeSoto Dealership

In 1929, John T. Waters and his brother James F. Waters founded the James F. Waters Inc Desoto-Plymouth dealership in San Francisco, California. Originally from Waterbury, Connecticut, the brothers were in the used car business for a short time before opening up their DeSoto-Plymouth dealership on the corner of Bush and Van Ness. In the early 1930s, brothers William and Robert Waters came out to join John and James in the new family business and, within a short time, the Waters had built the largest DeSoto-Plymouth dealership in the world. A second DeSoto-Plymouth dealership was opened in Long Island City, New York, next to Manhattan.

Aside from normal production cars, the Waters brothers sold thousands of long wheelbase DeSoto taxis out of their twin dealerships. The cabs themselves were specifically converted to be taxis by a plant in Detroit owned by the Waters. New, long wheelbase sedans would be shipped, without glass, from Briggs Body in Detroit to the Waters plant at Greenfield Road. Waters would install a bucket

seat for the driver, a partition, and a leather rear seat with Pullman style jump seats sporting a "W" stamped in steel on the rear facing side. Most, if not all, cabs bound for New York City were equipped with a sliding sunroof unlike most California DeSoto taxis. Current thinking is that all of the big DeSoto taxis that came out of the Detroit plant were considered Skyviews even if there was no sunroof or Skyview signage. Special Waters top lights and roofside availability lights adorned many of the jumbo taxis, especially in Manhattan.

The four Waters brothers, William, John, James, and Robert, died respectively in 1936, 1941, 1944, and 1954, leading to liquidation soon after Robert's death. Coincidentally, Chrysler discontinued its long wheelbase sedans that same year, eliminating the possibility of more seven-passenger taxis. The San Francisco dealership building is still in use today as a Chevrolet outlet.

Waters dealership in San Francisco.

The Waters dealerships catered not only to DeSotos but also to any domestic four-door sedan with their Offset Taxicab Division insert that included a bucket seat and partition as one unit. After removing the front bench seat out of an ordinary sedan this unit would bolt in and turn a stock sedan into a legally conforming taxicab in a few minutes. A single, rear facing jump seat with the Waters' "W" on the back of it allowed four to sit in back at a cost of only $175 F.O.B. Detroit. *Chris Monier*

There was nothing small about the big DeSotos and with an overall length of 226 inches, they were about as long as a Cadillac limousine of the same year. With modest six-cylinder power moving two tons around, a Skyview wasn't about speed as much as comfort and longevity. With the Long Island James F. Waters DeSoto-Plymouth dealership in the background, this 1941 was showing off its special hubcaps that read "Waters" on them. *Nathan Willensky*

In places with cold winters like New York City, a popular accessory was the snap-on winterguard that blocked air to the radiator in an attempt to raise the temperature of the water and keep this 1941 DeSoto Skyview's huge passenger compartment from turning into a meat locker. You can tell that this is a New York State taxi by the license number since it started with the letter "O," not the number zero. All New York State taxi plates at this time began with the letter "O" for "omnibus." *Peter Kanze*

San Francisco Yellow Cab owned this four-year-old 1941 DeSoto Skyview, Number 274. Like its East Coast cousins, it went through the James F. Waters DeSoto conversion plant in Detroit to get the interior touches like a partition and stamped "W"s on the jump seats. It is currently believed that few or none at all of the California DeSotos used a sunroof or the Skyview name. The bumper guards were different from the East Coast since they were probably fabricated locally. The location of the fleet number on the right front roof is unusual. Number 274 was missing its hood ornament. *San Francisco Public Library*

The rear of the same 1941 DeSoto Skyview displayed a trunk mounted ad sign that was typical for the period. The cab looked fairly stock except that the license plate and light were in an unusual location and, unlike their Manhattan counterparts, the trunks were functional so no luggage rack was required. *San Francisco Public Library*

There were a lot of big, yellow DeSotos serving San Francisco in 1944 and they used to line up like this batch outside of the train station at 3rd and Townsend Streets. San Francisco Yellow Cab had 503 licenses to operate and, chances are, each one was attached to a yellow jumbo. Compared to the somewhat beat up, dark DeSoto sedan with no hubcaps parked in the foreground, the true size of these Skyviews becomes apparent. None of the 1941 DeSotos in this picture had a sunroof. *San Francisco Public Library*

For the New York City market, Packard took its upscale One-Sixty seven-passenger sedan and stripped it down with One-Ten trim to minimize unwanted chrome for a vehicle that everybody knew was going to get banged up in traffic. The 3,950-lb cab was, appropriately enough, called the New York Taxi and it featured all the goodies required by law: trunk rack, license plate up on the trunklid, and five-in-the-rear seating with privacy partition. A sunroof was installed over the leather-trimmed rear compartment and a Packard crest decal looked sharp on the rear doors. Even though this body style normally had an eight-cylinder engine, a six-cyl-

inder flathead moved this taxi feast around town although the eight's larger radiator and other heavy-duty features were retained to help the overworked six cope under severe conditions. It is currently unknown how many of these New York taxis were produced in 1941 and 1942. None are thought to exist today. *Nathan Willensky*

A relatively rare taxi when new, only 756 1942 DeSoto DeLuxe taxis were produced before World War II curtailed all taxicab production. What set them apart from the DeSotos before and after them is the way the headlights were hidden behind crank-open doors. At that time, only the coffin-nosed Cords had that kind of thing so it was a very avant-garde stylings move for sedate DeSoto to undertake. Considering that DeSoto sold less than 100 private, long wheelbase cars in 1942, the 756 taxis must have helped justify the continuation of that body style. This DeSoto Skyview had a sunroof, some large bumper guards, and fog lights. The roof light is unusual. Judging from all the extras on this car, it was most likely an owner-operator unit. *DaimlerChrysler*

The rear of this damaged 1942 DeSoto Skyview from Manhattan shows how the rear trunk rack fit over the rear bumper guards. The screw-on plates that read "Skyview" above the trunklid and along the sides of the roof were nice touches. *Oldee Taxi Instruments*

1942 DeSoto Skyview- view of headlights open
Oldee Taxi Instruments

From this view of the same car, it appears that this 1942 DeSoto Skyview was hit hard in the right and then rolled. The flat spots on the end of the hood and the front of the roof must have been landing points. The enormous outer bumper guards don't fit the bumper very well but they look ready to sack the unwary slowpoke. It was normal practice for fleets to permanently make the headlight doors remain open due to problems with the opening mechanisms after a couple smash-ups. None of these big 1942 taxis are known to be around today. *Oldee Taxi Instruments*

A National Transportation Checker Model A waited for a fare in Manhattan during WWII. The headlights on this cab were quite dark and could possibly have been darkened to aid in the dimming down of the city's lights at night to make it less off a glowing target for marauding German U boats. Dimouts were a common event in New York City during this time and it meant no display or unneccessary lighting after dusk. To save steel for the war effort, this Checker was also missing its front license plate and metal operating medallion- a paper permit in the windshield filled in as a wartime subsitute. *Nathan Willensky*

When the new 120-inch wheelbase Packard Clipper Series 2100 came out in 1946, it was immediately turned into a cab. Like the units before World War II, you could have a taxi with a front bench seat or a bucket seat with an offset partition. It is currently unknown if any long-wheelbase taxis were constructed this year. Unlike most Packards this year, taxis used six-cylinder engines with three-speed manual transmissions. The Packard crest on the rear door looked classy. *Roger and Linda Lamm*

The interior of the 1947 Packard taxi had leather seats with a vinyl headliner. An access panel in the headliner, over the driver's seat, allowed for work on the roof light from below. *Roger and Linda Lamm*

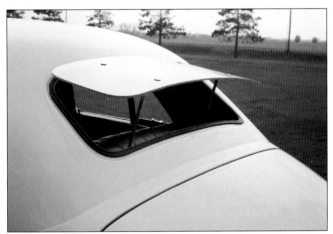

Unlike the 1941 and 1942 Packard New York Cabs, no postwar Packard taxis had sunroofs and no more were planned. To help mitigate this loss, windshield wiper maker Trico had a vacuum operated rear window opening device that worked via a mechanism in the trunk as standard equipment. It would pivot the back glass out from the bottom and allow for ventilation thoughout the cab. *Roger and Linda Lamm*

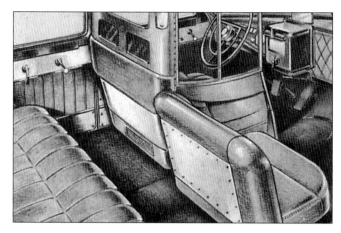

The interior of the Clipper Cab could hold three in the rear seat and perhaps one or two more in the folding jump seat when equipped with a partition. *Henry Winningham*

George Brodie, assistant to the President of Packard Motors, sat in the jump seat while Sam Abramson of the Yale Taxi Company of New York City was seated in the rear. There was talk of allowing this seating arrangement in Manhattan but few, if any, were allowed there before the Hack Bureau said no. *Nathan Willensky*

The postwar DeSoto retained the basic styling it had been wearing when hostilities broke out in 1942, except that many of the body parts were a little different and the headlights were now exposed. The engine was still essentially the prewar flathead six displacing 237 cubic inches and cranking out 109 horsepower. Even though there were semi-automatic transmissions available from DeSoto this year, cabbies stuck with the tried-and-true three-speed stick shifts and column shifters. DeSoto normally put all their cabs in their entry-level DeLuxe series and as many as 11,600 of the long wheelbase Skyviews were built with a majority going to California. The percentage of New York Skyviews with a sunroof seems to be about half but true numbers are unknown. A few 1946 to 1948 specimens are left for us to enjoy. This 1946 DeSoto Skyview was photographed in New York City but it currently resides in France. *Chris Monier*

Right after World War II, quite a few returning veterans wished to drive cabs but not all of them could get permission to operate since the number of cab licenses was frozen in many major cities. Licenses would eventually become available but to get by in the interim period some vets operated free cabs and worked for tips in order to avoid the designation of a "for hire" taxicab. This particular scene is of a War Veterans' Taxicab Association cab in Los Angeles, California. 142 vets paid $2,000 apiece to form this company. The cab itself is a 1938 Buick Century that has been made into a taxi with the addition of some two-tone paint, door decals, a couple of roof lights, and plaid seat covers. Used luxury cars made good cabs because they had lots of room for people, their mileage was usually low, and few wanted them so they were cheap. *Nathan Willensky*

The Veterans Cab Company in San Francisco had at least one 1946 Mercury Town Sedan taxi and it is shown here in 1948 parked at the intersection of Golden Gate and Jones Streets. The cab had a divider window and meter lights. The standard engine in Mercurys was a flathead, 239 V-8 with a three-speed transmission. While not nearly as popular a taxi as its six-cylinder Ford cousin, Mercury battled it out with mostly Pontiacs, Oldsmobiles, and regular wheelbase DeSotos for the small, higher priced segment of the taxi market. *San Francisco Public Library*

A DeSoto Skyview with a sunroof poses on a Manhattan street. The Gates Service Corporation operated it and their logo on the rear doors was a whitewall tire sitting above some wings. The interior had the bucket seat and partition as required by law and the front bumper guards are noteworthy since they wrap around the corners. Dealers and meter shops normally installed aftermarket bumper guards. This Gates DeSoto may not be around today but the Optimo Cigar Company is still serving New Yorkers. *Nathan Willensky*

An armed guard looks like he wanted to give the lady passenger of this sanitary 1946 to 1948 DeSoto Skyview a red tape parade but, in reality, this was just a New York City movie set for the 1953 movie *Taxi*, starring actor Dan Dailey. Of interest is the hole in the right front cowl since that's where the taxi medallions used to be. By 1953, it had moved to the hood as on this car. This cab is in good shape for its age so it probably had a meticulous owner-operator who kept after it. A fleet cab can have many different drivers in one week while a private owner might have just themselves and one other trustworthy individual allowed behind the wheel. *Chris Monier*

Anybody wondering if DeSoto could have built over 11,000 long wheelbase taxis during this time period didn't need to look very long at the inside of this fleet garage in Los Angeles to find an answer. All of the multi-colored 1946 to 1948 DeSotos in for service were jumbo Skyview models without sunroofs. Los Angeles Yellow Cab operated 1,200 cabs, making it the third largest fleet in the country at that time. It is no coincidence that Los Angeles Yellow Cab and San Francisco Yellow Cab used the same types of cabs since they had the same owner, W. Lansing Rothschild. *Nathan Willensky*

This New York City fleet of DeSoto Skyviews was reposing out in the open because most fleet cabs never saw a garage unless they were broken. With a life span of only two or three years, taxis didn't hang around long enough to get rusty. Fleet cabs with some life left in them were regularly sold to small towns or other cities. As this view illustrates, only about half of these taxis had the sunroof option. The factor that determined which car got a hole in the roof and which didn't is currently unknown. By this time, Packard and Checker had quit making open air cabs so DeSoto was quite alone. For paying passengers, the 1948 models would be the end of a great era in open sunroof taxi riding. *Henry Winningham*

Two classic modes of public transportation that were well built, durable, and easy on the eye: A GM bus and an old DeSoto! *Chris Monier*

New Yorkers had something special with their sunroof-equipped DeSoto Skyviews and nothing has replaced them yet. Between the leather seats and the view out of the top, it makes all the cabs since then look positively austere. Normal flooring was a rubberized matting, unlike the carpeting in this restored example, and the air duct tubes running along the sides of the partition were added recently for air conditioning. *Richard DeLuna*

Chevrolet Stylemaster cabs were only slightly changed from their 1942 predecessors but postwar demand was so high that Chevrolet was selling every cab it could build. A small town in Illinois used postwar Stylemasters equipped with a bucket seat and partition. It's possible that the bucket seat may have been installed by GM considering their ample supply of such seats for their sedan delivery lines, but the partition is most likely an aftermarket. Another estimate is that the whole seat and divider could have been a universal type insert designed to fit most large American sedans. This driver looks very official in her uniform. *Henry Winningham*

Condensed Specifications

Engine: L-Head, 6 cylinders, 105 B.H.P. @ 3600 RPM. Removable precision type main and connecting rod bearings.

Engine Lubrication: Full pressure lubrication to all main, connecting rod, camshaft and piston pin bearings, also to valve tappets.

Fuel System: Single tube down-draft carburetor, automatic choke, automatic heat control, idling control, pump with filter.

Clutch: Special semi-centrifugal single dry plate type 11 inch diameter. Ball throw-out bearing, permanently lubricated.

Transmission: Synchronized, carburized, helically cut gears, 9 ball and roller bearings.

Frame: X-member type frame, box section side rails.

Brakes: Packard Servo-Hydraulic, oversize self-energizing type service brakes. Mechanical handbrake operating rear wheel brake shoes.

Steering System: Worm and three tooth roller type gear, mounted on double row needle bearings and two tapered roller bearings, 21 ft. turning radius.

Wheelbase: 120 inches.

Bodies: All steel body, safety glass throughout. Genuine leather upholstery, partition or sedan type seating.

Standard Equipment: Twin horns, driver's sun visor, double two-speed electric windshield wipers, door rear-view mirror, special outside bonnet lock, power operated rear window, rear compartment reading light, two combination stop and tail lights, new side-guard bumpers and guards front and rear.

PACKARD *Clipper* CAB
ASK THE MAN WHO OWNS ONE
PACKARD MOTOR CAB COMPANY • DETROIT 32, MICHIGAN

The 1946 to 1947 Packard Series 2100 taxis sold new for $1,945. No long wheelbase New York models are thought to have been built in this series.

1948 Checker A2 NYC- postcard *Chris Monier*

The new Checker Model A2 debuted in 1948 wearing contemporary styling with only one body style and one wheelbase. With an overall length of 206 inches and a wheelbase of 124 inches, the A2 was about as long as a regular wheelbase DeSoto but had jump seats and could carry five in the rear. At 3,650 lbs, the new Checker was about 300 lbs lighter than a big DeSoto and a substantial 800 lbs less weighty than Packard's 1948 New York model. This particular cab was painted ivory with a green top and belonged to the Checker owned National Transportation Company in New York City. The whitewalls were an unlikely fleet option. *Joe Fay*

A strike at New York City's National Transportation idled a huge number of Model A2 Checkers and they were locked up tight. Of interest on these cabs were the mirrors on the right front fenders and the leather belts wrapped around the trunk racks. The new Checker came with a Continental flathead six-cylinder engine displacing 226 cubic inches with a three-speed manual transmission as the only available shifting option. *Corbis*

A 1948 Checker Model A2 waited at the same light in Manhattan as a Gates DeSoto did in an earlier picture. This profile shows the fluid lines of the new styling and the large passenger compartment that allowed enough space for rectangular jump seats. Nearly all Model A2s came with bucket seats and partitions whereas its companion sedan, the Checker A3, had a full front bench seat and no divider. This Model A2 belonged to the Yellow Taxi System and wears the optional hood ornament and chrome rear fender guards. The front bumper's standard two guards were supplemented by an additional pair for maximum grille protection. *Nathan Willensky*

Chicago Checker Cab ordered up some new 1948 Model A2s in green and ivory. Since it was a Chicago Checker, it had to have their trademark checkerboard decal, although the treatment where the stripes peter out on the hood is unusual. The optional hood ornament and chrome rear gravel shields made the cab look distinguished. While Checker produced nearly 6,000 A2 taxis from February 1947 to May 1950, perhaps two or three restorable examples remain in Finland. A large number of well used, ex-Chicago Checker Model A2s were shipped to Helsinki around 1950 for the Olympics, and a few remain today. *Ben Merkel*

Jump seats had been a Checker hallmark since the beginning and the Model A2 came with them unless they were specifically deleted. While not as fancy as years past, the rear interior was done up in a tough vinyl with rubber floor mats, which were handy for cities that might have required a taxi to be hosed out every night. *Ben Merkel*

With Buick out of the cab business, Packard was the last prestige player in town. It was quite something for Packard to have been able to market a decontented luxury car to cab fleets and compete with bread and butter taxis like Chevrolet and Plymouth for good old American urban turf. This well dressed driver looks pretty pleased to be driving this upscale Packard Twenty-Second Series for Boston Checker Cab. Note the Packard factory roof light that was ordered to read "Checker." Boston requires a Hackney Carraige License to operate and on this Packard it's seen just to the right of the left headlight. *Oldee Taxi Instruments*

The Plymouth DeLuxe taxi for 1949 was all new except for its flathead six engine. The boxy design was sedate but functional and that's what many of the cab fleets wanted. Since Plymouth made its last long wheelbase sedan in 1942, only one four-door sedan was available for cab service. Priced at around $1,500, they sold well. The pictured taxi belonged to Cincinnati, Ohio, Yellow Cab. The trunklid mounted circular advertising sign was typical for the period. The plastic taxi dome was also a fairly common sight by now and was far more effective than the old fashioned three clearance lights for the major reason that you could put your name and phone number up where the public could see it. The two lights on the side of the roof are meter lights. *Nathan Willensky*

The 1948 Twenty-Second Series Packard New York Taxi was built using the 226-inch Super Eight seven passenger sedan as a base. These long bodies were built for Packard by professional car builder Henney Corporation of Freeport, Illinois and featured the bucket seat and partition arrangement that was required by law. With only a 105 horsepower six cylinder under the hood, the 4,460 lbs taxi didn't move quickly. Approximately 1,316 were constructed in 1948 but numbers dropped drastically in 1949 and 1950 and there were no taxis in the 1951 line up. These New York Taxis were decommissioned. *Nathan Willensky*

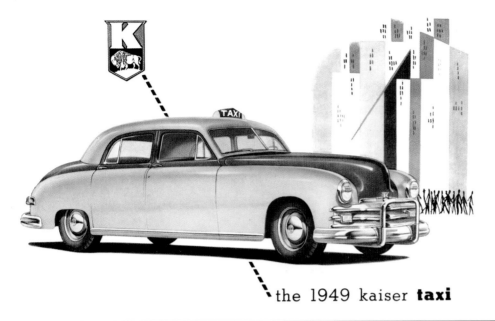

the 1949 kaiser **taxi**

It seems that everybody wanted to get in on the taxi action and Kaiser-Frazer Corporation was no exception. Their 1949 taxi featured an all vinyl interior with aluminum kick panels at the bottom of all four doors. The engine was a 226-ci Continental six-cylinder flathead with a 10-inch-diameter clutch and its mission was to move 3,345 lbs of Kaiser around town. Heavy-duty springs and shock absorbers finished the basic taxi package. The large, tubular front bumper guard on the cab in this picture was optional, as was the "Taxi" roof light. It is unknown how many of these cabs were sold but it was probably not a lot. None have turned up so they might all be gone. *Linda Danzig*

In May 1950, Checker came out with a revised version of their A2 taxi and called it, predictably enough, the A4. While it may have looked a lot like the A2, almost everything was different, from the size of the rear window to the bumpers and to the fenders. The chrome beltline trim was dropped as was the hood trim reaching down to the grille. This Model A4 was parked at the home of Morris Markin, Checker's founder. His house is just a few miles from the factory in Kalamazoo, Michigan, and is now a park. *Ben Merkel*

To appreciate the subtle differences between the A2 and A4, this profile should be compared to the 1948 A2 profile shown earlier. The pontoon extension on the front doors was bolted on and when the cabs got rusty these would fall off without notice. Power was from a 226-ci Continental six-cylinder flathead that was close to, but not the same as, those used in some Willys and Kaisers. The only official transmission available was a three-speed stick shift but some automatics may have been installed by special order. *Ben Merkel*

Checker followed Packard's lead and offered a Trico Lite Lift for the back glass as standard equipment and a fixed window became optional. With the touch of a button in the driver's area, the glass would pivot out allowing for ventilation on a hot day. The lifting mechanism was mounted in the trunk. *Ben Merkel*

A view of the Trico Lite Lift mechanism. *Ben Merkel*

A large batch of fresh Checker A4s dutifully sat at the factory awaiting transport to Chicago Yellow Cab. From June 1950 to October 1952, Checker built 6,383 Model A4 taxis and companion A5 sedans with most being the former and not the latter. In 1950, the average Chicago cab on the Loop ran up 300 miles per day and the expected life of a cab there was only two or three years. *Ben Merkel*

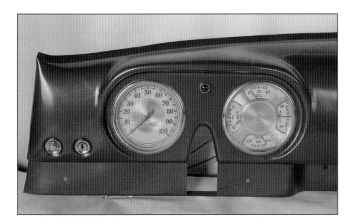

A 1950 Model A4 instrument cluster. *Ben Merkel*

Checker's A4 had a contoured rear seat that was quite comfortable. Vinyl was used for the upholstery and the flooring was rubber matting that looked like carpet. Some Checkers were ordered with the same one-piece Formica flooring that might be found in a kitchen. The flaps halfway up the doors were designed to keep fingers and clothing out of the door hinge area. These finger guards were required in some places like New York City. Interior colors were either gray and blue or red and brown. *Ben Merkel*

In the days before antifreeze was universally used, it wasn't unusual for cab companies in cold climates to either drain the radiators every night or let the taxis idle all night as these Checker Model A4s were doing in Chicago. *Henry Winningham*

Out of over 6,000 A4 taxis built, this unrestored example is the only one known of in the States at this time. MGM Studios, among others, kept a lot of old taxis until the early 1970s when they were auctioned off and this is one of those cars. A project A4 exists in Finland. *Ben Merkel*

This pleasing front view of a 1950 Checker A4 shows the intricate grille that a cab company tried to protect by welding a pipe between the bumper guards. The second grille tooth from the top right is the latch used to open the hood. *Ben Merkel*

Americans have always had a facination for English taxis and every couple of years a few cabbies gave them a shake. In 1950, an Austin cab was tried out in New York City and it seemed to be attracting a lot of attention from other drivers as they took exaggerated notice of the length difference between the Yank Tank and its English visitor. The DeSoto was notable for its unusual bumper guard and medallion placement in the small spot between the right front door and hood. Its fleet number, 303, was stenciled right on the front of the cab. It looks like someone took the medallion off of the Austin because there's a hole in the cowl where it would most likely have been. *Nathan Willensky*

A very pretty 1950 DeSoto Skyview posed inside a New York City parking garage. Since the design change in 1949 to the new square look, no DeSotos Skyviews were built with sunroofs even if they said "Skyview" all over them. These gigantic DeSotos were the 4,200-lb gorillas of the taxi world now that Packard was leaving the cab business. By contrast, a 1950 Checker A4 weighed almost 600 lbs less. For cab drivers in Manhatten after 1950, they either drove a Checker or a DeSoto because only those two still made a taxi that could meet New York City's five-in-the-rear ordinance. Only 680 DeSoto taxis were built in 1949 and 2,350 in 1950. *Nathan Willensky*

With thousands of cab companies serving small towns and cities everywhere, it was regular practice for cabbies to purchase new taxis from the strongest car dealer in the area in order to take advantage of the parts and service facilities. Ford, with its major class dealer network, had a 1950 DeLuxe four-door sedan with a taxi package that was quite close to the police package and it consisted of heavy-duty suspension, brakes, clutch, radiator, seat springs, and vinyl upholstery. Like the Plymouth, it was priced close to $1,500 with the flathead six-cylinder engine and three-speed manual transmission. *Chris Monier*

The first 1950 Studebaker Champion DeLuxe taxi in San Francisco was sold to the Luxor Cab Company. The Studebaker weighed only 2,750 lbs so the 85-hp flathead six had adequate power. The styling of the new Studebakers was big news for 1950 and they sold a lot of cars with it. *San Francisco Public Library*

In 1951, the intersection of 42nd Street and Broadway looked like this. The orange and white Checker A4 in the foreground worked for Empire Cab and it had the Empire State Building on its rear door logo. The DeSoto to the right of it was an orange Terminal Cab, which had a dachshund with the name "Wags" on its rear door. Apparently, Wags was a real dog that belonged to the wife of the cab company owner. Of interest is the 1950 Chevrolet DeLuxe Styleline station wagon passing through the intersection because it was one of those experiments that didn't result in any large fleet buys. Station wagon taxis were nothing new in Manhattan as Checker had a nine-passenger station wagon approved for cab use back in 1931. *Nathan Willensky*

The Checker Cab Company in Boston ordered up some Plymouth Cambridge taxis in 1951. The attributes of Plymouth's solid but conservative design were obvious to fleet operators: Reliable flathead six-cylinder motor in a boxy 3,100-lb cab that could haul six adults. This Boston taxi had a full front seat and a partition so its passenger capacity was limited to three. The reality is that most taxi trips involve fewer than two people so three was a winner most of the time. Boston Checker still used the old metal and glass roof lights and transferred them from cab to cab. Some of the older metal roof lights were so crowned for the old, round roofs that they couldn't fit the newer flat ones. The Hackney license number seen on the end of the hood had no relation to either the fleet number of this Plymouth or the license plate digits. *Oldee Taxi Instruments*

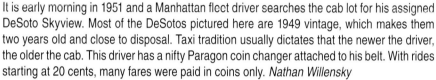

It is early morning in 1951 and a Manhattan fleet driver searches the cab lot for his assigned DeSoto Skyview. Most of the DeSotos pictured here are 1949 vintage, which makes them two years old and close to disposal. Taxi tradition usually dictates that the newer the driver, the older the cab. This driver has a nifty Paragon coin changer attached to his belt. With rides starting at 20 cents, many fares were paid in coins only. *Nathan Willensky*

This driver must have had a good record as "upstairs" slipped him a new 1951 DeSoto Skyview to take out on his rounds. Wearing Skyview trim, it was now in name only as there was no longer a sunroof option. The cautious driver checked his equipment before heading out. *Nathan Willensky*

For drivers, a brand new fleet taxi is a treat. Since new cab euphoria doesn't last very long, this man was going to make the most of this fresh Skyview by making it perfect and appealing. Somebody put aftermarket chome eyelids over the headlights to give it a newer look. The sturdy looking bumper guard was needed since the DeSoto's chrome teeth were fairly vulnerable. Chrome aerials stick out from both front fenders so a driver could see where the corners were. The fleet owner probably put them on in a futile attempt to keep the sheet-metal pristine. The operating medallion was moved to the hood on this car because there was no longer a space between the hood and front doors. Here it would stay. *Oldee Taxi Instruments*

The fleet driver glided through Central Park and passed a relic from another time, a horse-drawn carriage. Today, carriages still ply Cental Park but no trace remains of the old DeSotos. *Nathan Willensky*

It was nighttime in Times Square and the fleet driver was trolling for fares using the gleaming DeSoto as 4,500 lbs of live bait. *Oldee Taxi Instruments*

Once long ago, three generations of DeSoto Skyviews stopped for a light in New York City. The left front cab was a 1940 with a sunroof, remarkable that it survived the World War II period and was now 11 years old! A fussy owner-operator no doubt owned it. Behind it was a postwar 1946 to 1948 DeSoto with the larger back glass, taillights, and a sunroof. The final Mopar under inspection was the newest one on the right, probably a 1951, which had no hole in its roof. The Chevrolet Staton Wagon taxi in the point position was part of a small, experimental fleet in the early 1950s. *Nathan Willensky*

The only known DeSoto Skyview from the 1949 to 1954 period is this unrestored 1952 example, photographed at the pier in Le Havre, France, in 2005. A flathead, 116-hp, six-cylinder motor and three-speed manual transmission were the normal drivetrain combination found in these mammoth cabs. The roof light on this car is a much later plastic unit. 3,550 DeSoto taxis were built from 1951 to 1952. *Claude Brami*

For a Manhattan DeSoto Skyview driver in 1952, it was no picnic to spend a 10-hour shift behind the wheel. Not only did operators have to deal with a large, ivory plastic steering wheel that was almost up against their chest but they also had to endure a very uncomfortable bucket seat. As usual, luggage could go up front next to the driver, in back with the passengers, or lashed to the trunk rack. *Claude Brami*

The large, Ohmer meter in this subject 1952 DeSoto sits on a platform attached to the partition and prints a receipt. Some meters from this period were mounted on stands coming out of the floor so that passengers could read them easily from the rear compartment. *Claude Brami*

With their new model only three years away, Checker opted to facelift the old 1948 body style one more time before termination. The new cab, known as the Model A6, confined most of the major exterior changes to a higher roof and simpler, stamped grille to replace the intricate A4 affair. Production began in January 1953 and ended in December 1954. While production numbers are sketchy, 6,000 or so were built but only one very poor example is known to exist today and it resides in Finland. No Checkers were built in 1955 while the plant retooled for a totally new car. *Henry Winningham*

Only in this view can the higher rear roof on the 1953 A6 be discernable. The hubcaps became a bit more pronounced than those on the previous A4. The same 226-ci Continental six-cylinder engine was hiding under the hood. Base price for an A6 was $2,458.20. *Ben Merkel*

The checkerboard on the front of this A6's hood had a thicker border on the bottom than on the top. Not all A6s had this kind of decal so it's unknown which cabs got the even border and which ones got the one shown here. *Ben Merkel*

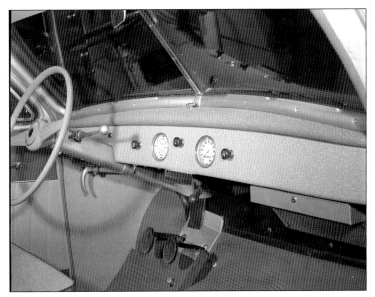

The dashboard of the 1953 A6 was very different from the A4 and it marked the first time Checker tried "idiot lights" instead of gauges for the oil pressure and ammeter. Their experience must have been poor as Checker went back to gauges in 1956 and didn't try warning lights again until 1973. Checker was falling behind its competitors by not offering power accessories and automatic transmissions. They would catch up soon, however. *Ben Merkel*

By 1952, Checker's A4 pontoon design was beginning to look a little dated. Checker Cab Manufacturing was thinking of the future and proposed this clay model in 1952 as possibly the 1953 Checker. The roofline was fairly close to what would emerge with the all-new 1956 A8. *Ben Merkel*

Somebody at Boston Checker Cab wanted to promote safe driving with this interesting 1953 Plymouth Cambridge. Since Boston Checker bought a lot of cars from Plymouth, maybe it was a freebie? It could also have been a clean, used cab that somebody at Checker Cab had painted for a lark. Regardless of its origin, somebody at the company probably drove the car as a courtesy car, since it had no meter or taxi roof light. Despite the best of intentions, the paint job on this sturdy, little Plymouth probably caused more accidents than it prevented! *Oldee Taxi Instruments*

Boston's Checker Taxi Company operated this 1953 Dodge Meadowbrook taxi equipped with a 230 cubic inch flathead six and three speed manual transmission. While not as popular a cab as Plymouth, Dodge remained a strong contender in the taxi market with styling that was equal to GM and Ford's cab offerings but ahead of Checker's postwar fastback body. With a weight of about 3,200 lbs, Dodge's taxi was fairly light and economical. Inside, three passengers could sit behind a full partition with large, chrome grab handles on each end. The checkerboard decal treatment on the trunklid was unusual and well executed. *Oldee Taxi Instruments*

The 1953 Checker A6 had an interior that was hard to hurt. The seats were upholstered in a textured vinyl that was the same material trucks and school buses were using at the time. The floors were either rubberized matting or one sheet of Formica in the rear. The woman seated was Mrs. Ward C. Morgan, the photographer's wife. *Ben Merkel*

Chicago, Illinois, was a Checker town for a long time primarily because Checker Cab Manufacturing owned the two biggest fleets there, the Checker and Yellow Cab companies. When Manhattan was awash with DeSotos and Checkers, Chicago was swimming in mostly Checkers. Luckily, both brands were good so everybody won. A look north up Michigan Avenue from Lake Street on September 5, 1955, revealed a pair of Model A6 Chicago Checker Cabs cruising past with a couple of Chicago Yellows behind them. The location of the front license plate on the end of the hood was odd but that placement seemed to be normal for all of Chicago's Checkers at that time. *Henry Winningham*

Another A6 Chicago Checker Cab shows off the green and ivory paint colors still used today. A bucket seat and partition still comprised the most common A6 interior configuration but change was afoot and within a few years it would all be different. *Chris Monier*

34 Years of Safe, Courteous, and Responsible Service

Two legendary taxis, a 1953 Checker A6 and a 1951 DeSoto Skyview, tangled in Manhattan traffic back in 1954 when they tried to occupy the same space. Note how the fleet number is stenciled onto the front fender near the headlight. *Chris Monier*

A worker is seen here applying a checkerboard decal at the factory. *Jane McCowan*

Several Chicago Checker A6 cabs are seen here under construction at the factory. *Jane McCowan*

One of the most important dates in New York City taxi history is July 16, 1954, because that was the day New York City allowed regular sedans to be taxis. At a ceremony in front of the Hack Bureau at 156 Greenwich Street, three new "small" cabs wait for the green light: A 1953 Chevrolet, a 1954 Plymouth, and a 1954 Ford. The 1954 Dodge was about to be approved but it missed the festivities. DeSoto Skyviews began to disappear rapidly as nearly every fleet owner in town began pitting Ford, General Motors, and Chrysler dealers against each other for the cheapest taxi prices. *Nathan Willensky*

At the intersection of Greenwich and Cortland Streets in Manhattan, history was made when this newly approved 1954 Ford Customline taxi cruised out of the Hack Bureau carrying officials for the maiden voyage. Of importance is the fact that there was not a partition or bucket seat in this car. Since 1952, you could use trunks again so there was no longer a need for luggage space up front. For its day, the Ford wasn't a small car but, when compared to this DeSoto, it looked like a compact! The Ford's bumper guards were quite comprehensive. *Nathan Willensky*

Over in Kalamazoo, Michigan, home of Checker Cab Manufacturing, the final form of their new car was almost completed. Due out in 1956, it was going to have to be a winner. At that time, nobody could have known and nobody would have believed that the basic upcoming body would be in production until 1982. *Ben Merkel*

A Checker A6 came down the assembly line in Kalamazoo in 1954. Its destination was the Checker-owned National Transportation Company in New York City and it already had the rate stickers on the front doors and the National decals on the rear. *Ben Merkel*

The Checker Model A6 was available in an endless variety of color combinations as these four profiles show. With the large number of cab operators across the U.S. in the early 1950s, few fleet color schemes were unique to one company.

A sampling of some of the fleets Circa 1954

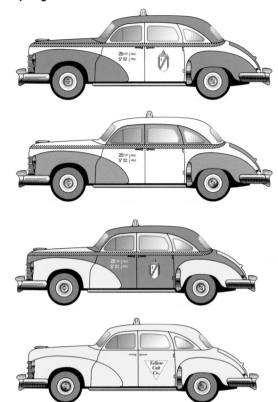

On June 16, 1954, an impressive show was put on to celebrate the opening of the Chrysler Proving Grounds near Chelsea, Michigan. A total of 22 brand new Plymouth taxis were delivered to top drivers from 22 different cab companies and each one was treated as Chrysler's guest. The first two were going to Yellow Cab and Fleetway Cab, of Baltimore, Maryland, the third to Whitman's Black and White Cab of Birmingham, Alabama and the fourth and fifth to Boston Checker Cab and Boston Cab in Massachussetts. Chrysler liked to brag that there were more Plymouth taxis on the road in America than all other taxi brands combined, and they were probably correct. *Nathan Willensky*

1955 to 2005

Pressure had been building to allow regular, production line taxis for years in places like New York City and the final moment came on July 16, 1954, when the city approved Chevrolet, Ford, Plymouth, and Dodge four-door sedans for use as taxis in a ceremony at the Hack Bureau. Conspicuously absent was DeSoto who, after serving Gotham for decades, quietly discontinued their long wheelbase models and left the taxi making business until 1957 when it came back briefly for a two year encore before vanishing for the last time. Checker was, by default, the last cab with jump seats but they didn't make any cars in 1955 while they tooled up for their new offering in 1956. Not only were the limousine cabs put out to pasture but many of the old rules concerning them such as non-functioning trunk and bumper rack were sacked too. Within a short time, there were suddenly a lot of Ford and Dodge taxis rocketing through Times Square.

The new, "small" taxis were a huge leap forward in terms of drivability and driver comfort with the addition of such taxi novelties as fully automatic transmission, power steering, and brakes in a car with 30 percent less exterior bulk and a cheaper price tag. Compared to the meatgrinder that had been the former taxi driving experience, one drive in a modern cab was enough to make drivers quip "Driver fatique, what's that?" It was found that cabbies could function longer with all these new effort-saving devices and the 1954 to 1956 period probably represented the biggest leap forward in driver stamina since the front seat was enclosed from the elements some 35 years earlier. By the late 1950s, the list of approved vehicles for taxi service in Manhattan had expanded to include such fresh faces as Rambler, Studebaker, Mercury, Buick, and even a few Mercedes. Some drivers refused to give up their pre-1955 DeSoto and Checker gunboats, however, and a small number of stalwart owner-operators were still making money with them until the early 1960s.

For passengers used to acres of leather, jumpseats, and room for all their friends, things weren't going so well. With the exception of Checker, a ride in the rear of your average 1956 basic fleet sedan wasn't like the old days at all. By this time, taxicabs and police cars were drawing off the same parts bin so any hint of luxury was omitted to keep costs down. A transmission hump now protruded into the passenger compartment of most cars and the middle passenger has had to deal with it ever since. Seats, formerly leather or countoured, had become shapeless slabs of foam covered with a vinyl so basic that some resembled seat covers. The knees of the passengers were now close to the back of the

The new 1955 Plymouth Plaza taxis were a big leap from the stodgy 1954 models and very few parts could be shared between the two except for the 230-ci flathead six-cylinder motor. Plymouth sales almost doubled this year and cab sales were brisk. Boston Checker Cab had been into Plymouths for years and kept coming back for more. The checkerboard decal was interesting in how it came up from both sides and joined in the front of the hood. The metal and glass roof light is an oldie. Plazas were priced near $1,700 and weighed in at a svelte 3,129 lbs. For the first time, a Plymouth taxi was available with V-8 power but it is doubtful that many were ordered with it since most fleet owners are nervous about a V-8's gas mileage and potential for excessive speed. *Oldee Taxi Instruments*

front seat and that meant any kind of full partition stole real passenger room. Rear door openings weren't square anymore so getting in and out was rougher on the elderly and handicapped. The remarkably low 1957 and 1958 Detroit offerings made the fare's situation worse by sinking the passenger compartments further into the frame in the interest of space age styling. Floors became pockets and the raised doorsill was and still is a dandy place for an exiting passenger to get hung up. Any liquid in this floor area had to be mopped out since it could not drain. The big manufacturers tried to make these interiors more user friendly by adding assist straps and door pull handles but they couldn't make much more space appear. Studebaker, in 1956, tried to maximize rear passenger room by using their largest 120.5-inch wheelbase sedan as the base for their taxi model in a noble effort to squeeze out a few more inches for the folks paying the tab. The public had little choice but to get used to it since Checker was being routinely outsold by Ford and Dodge

The 1956 Plymouth taxi could handle three passengers comfortably.
Ben Merkel

in major markets like New York City, and it was becoming harder and harder to grab one.

Checker's new A8 model came out, after at least a six-year development, in early 1956 and shared no parts with its predecessor except the Continental flathead engine, hood ornament, and glove box. Boxy and slab-sided, the new car gleaned its ball-joint front suspension, and automatic transmission from the 1954 Ford. Almost everything else from the seats to body stampings were manufactured in-house. Checker managed to keep an eight-passenger capacity within the exterior dimensions of a normal car by using two round jump seats aimed at a 45-degree angles to the right. Like the old models, fenders were bolted on, not welded, and servicability was stressed as bumpers were interchangable and the grille was an easily removed, stamped steel affair. Nobody could have known it at the time, but this was the last big body change that Checker would ever make. A modest restyle in 1958 to four headlights represented the final attempt at staying modern. For paying passengers, the old school Checker offered the last bastion of real legroom and folks lapped it up, when they could, by frequently bypassing stock sedan taxis in order to hail what they perceived as the last real taxi deal. This behavior continued for decades until Checkers came off the streets in the late 1980s.

Taxi operators didn't mind the new cabs since they were fairly cheap to buy and operate. They didn't have to worry about oddball limousine body parts anymore and the durable, overhead valve six cylinders from Ford and Chevy performed like older V-8s and gave better fuel economy. Air conditioning was another major option that began showing up in taxis, either built in to the dashboard from the factory or added on by a dealer later. It was welcomed by those cabbies that could afford its expensive initial purchase and upkeep. Most northeastern cities didn't make air conditioning mandatory until the mid 1980s but it was pretty common in southern and western cabs by 1973. In tourist cities, it was not unusual to find a requirement that only cabs with working air conditioning could pick up at the airport. The driver was now complete: Power brakes, power steering, automatic transmission, and temperature-controlled environment. Other than modern safety and navigational devices, not much has changed in the taxi front seat since Eisenhower was President.

By 1959, all the big US carmakers had some pretty wild looking sedans on the market and they were all quite large. Studebaker and, to a lesser extent, Rambler, bucked the trend by offering compact taxis that were quite inexpensive to buy and operate. By the time the Lark taxi was introduced in 1959, Studebaker-Packard Corporation had already sold over 1,000 Economiler cabs in New York City alone. The Lark sold well, too, and was seen in many cities like Pittsburg, Kansas City, Cleveland, and Detroit where 20 experimental, diesel-powered Lark taxis were clattering around. Rambler and Studebaker's success with smaller cars was not lost on GM, Ford, and Chrysler as all three fielded compacts the following year, although few Corvairs, Falcons, or Valiants were ever put into taxi service. An official from Plymouth-DeSoto-Valiant division admitted in December 1960 that out of 8,700 Valiants built so far only two were doing service as taxicabs and the results over at Chevrolet and Ford were little better as no compact could gracefully handle a four-passenger airport run with multiple, large bags. In November of that same year, Chrysler killed off its now-pathetic DeSoto division and introduced the 225 slant-six-cylinder, overhead valve engine, an inline design that seemed to run forever with a little care.

A new size niche was created in 1962 when Chevrolet introduced its mid-sized Chevy II taxi to counteract Ford's new threat, the smaller Fairlane taxi, but it was still too early as few American cab operators had caught the downsizing bug yet. Intermediate cabs wouldn't really catch on until Chrysler came out with the right combination of room, economy, and low cost with the 1965 Plymouth Belvedere and Dodge Coronet taxis. The bulletproof 225-ci slant six motor was married to the rugged 727 Torqueflite automatic in a six-passenger car that weighed less than 3,200 lbs. To make their cabs irresistible, Chrysler sold them aggressively with rebates and "baker's dozen" deals where you bought ten cabs and got the eleventh for free. To clinch the deal, the Chrysler 50,000-mile warranty was further supplemented by some large dealers for an additional 25,000 miles at a time when most carmakers were only offering 12,000 miles. By 1969, Chrysler had upped its drivetrain coverage to 75,000 miles. Checker's warranty was good for 4,000 miles in 1965 and by 1969 it had gone up to 12,000 miles. This wasn't a reflection on Checker's build quality more than it was an example of how a large corporation could do things when they had enough volume to amortize costs. In 1965, Plymouth built over 70,000 Belvedere four-door sedans while Checker constructed only 6,136 cars total that same year, approximately 85 percent of them being taxis and the rest were private Marathons and airport limousines.

By the mid 1960s, some of America's urban areas had become quite dangerous and cab drivers began to complain. The most obvious solution was a bulletproof partition that seperated the driver from the passenger. Partitions up to that time had been, for the most part, not bulletproof and were built more for privacy. A lot of drivers didn't like them because they tended to push the operator close to the steering wheel and caused strange reflections at night. It also kept cabbies from talking it up with passengers and that could have translated into diminished tips. Passengers didn't like them because not only did they intrude on already marginal legroom but heat and air conditioning tended to stay with the driver unless they opened up the divider window, which subsequently defeated the purpose of a partition in the first place. Also, in hard stops or crashes with an unbelted fare, the passenger's collision with a partition was and is the cause for

1956 Checker rear view

many injuries to this day. Despite all this, sturdier partitions went into production and most big city fleets adopted them. Checker offered a total safety package on its 1965 offerings that began with a full, padded partition featuring thick, bulletproof glass and a vacuum-controlled window that went up and down. A small cash drawer was present to minimize a driver's contact with a shady character. Checker Motors, in an effort to make sure their partitions would work, either test shot them behind the factory or had a company called Materials Research Laboratories pump both .45 caliber and .357 magnum metal-piercing bullets into them at point-blank range. All the bullets did was bulge the metal on the other side! These beefy partitions added nearly 100 lbs to Checker's nearly two-ton curb weight.

Besides partitions small, round safes were bolted to the front floors of many fleet cabs accompanied by an exterior decal telling a would-be robber that the driver only carried a few bucks and that the big bills were locked in a safe with no key. While this looked good on paper, pointing at a safe and offering a few dollars to a high, gun-toting thug can end badly so not every cabbie stashed their cash in one. Bandit lights were another popular security accessory that normally flashed some lights on the roof in an attempt to attract police attention, although that could end badly too if a perp saw a

reflection of the taxi and its blinking lights in a store front window. Newer versions in New York City have a blinking amber light in front near the grille and one in the trunklid facing to the rear. Power rear door locks gave the driver the option of locking out a suspicous character. This was another taxi option required by law in some places.

The gas crunch of the 1970s saw a move towards smaller taxis like the Plymouth Volare, Ford Granada, and Chevrolet Chevelle. This was bad news for big cab makers like Checker and sales gradually dropped to the point where it was no longer viable to keep the classic cab in production. In 1982, Checker's last year as a carmaker, only 2,000 of the boxy cabs were produced. Once they were all sold, the phone rang off the hook for more but by that time it was over. Checker Motors is still in business as a stamping supplier to the big carmakers but efforts to bring out a new model were stillborn once the giant price tags for research, retooling, and federal regulatory requirements were factored in. Checker Motors even went so far as to stretch a Volkswagen Rabbit and a Chevrolet Citation into five- and seven-passenger cabs but neither of those experiments was satisfactory. Some of the other attempts included customized minivans, a stretched Mercury Marquis built by AHA of Canada, and a federalized English cab built in Mt.

After years of development, Checker Cab Manufacturing unleashed their totally new car, the Model A8. It was revealed in January 1956 amidst much fanfare and anticipation. Checker was the last cab with jump seats and they managed to pack eight-passenger capacity into a car only 200-inches long. Their secret was to make the passenger compartment a little longer than regular sedans and then install two round, folding seats that, when pulled out of the floor, aimed the jump seat passenger's legs at a 45-degree angle to the right. It was a snug setup but it worked for the next 26 years and kept Checker popular in areas where you charged by the person, not by the group. This restored A8 is painted in New York City fleet colors and currently resides in Pennsylvania. *Bruce Uhrich*

Clemens, Michigan, circa 1986, by a company called The London Coach Company, Inc. The current English taxi is available in the States but its price tag of around $44,000 will keep it a fairly rare sight. Today, only vans come close to replacing the rear interior room of a DeSoto Skyview or a Checker Cab.

For cabbies, the demise of the Checker was just the beginning of bad news. Chrysler discontinued their last front engined, rear-wheel-drive taxis, the Plymouth Gran Fury and Dodge Diplomat, in 1989 followed by GM's decision to kill off the large Caprice Classic, a very popular taxi, in 1996. This left Ford as the last traditional taxi maker in the US. In 2002, after prodding from New York City's Mayor Rudy Giuliani regarding the lack of rear legroom in cabs, Ford brought out its first built-for-the-purpose taxi since the 1930s by basing their Crown Victoria taxi model on the slightly stretched Lincoln Town Car. This extra couple of inches allowed for some much needed space in cabs equipped with a partition. At this time taxi companies all over America are using this special Crown Victoria, which

isn't sold to the public or police, so it's strictly for cabbies only. It is remarkable that any current US automaker would build such a unique car for a relatively small market but, unfortunately, Ford has indicated that the Crown Victoria will be phased out by the end of the decade.

Where the American taxi will go from here is up in the air. Certainly, minivans, SUVs, and smaller sedans, like the Chevrolet Impala and Ford Five Hundred, can take up where the classic cabs left off but there is no question that some of the old timers left big shoes to fill. Without a doubt, hybrid and alternative fuel taxis are going to come on strong in the coming years but few, if any, US automakers are going to spend the many millions of dollars it takes to build specialized taxis in small numbers. There are proposals on the drawing boards for all kinds of futuristic, for hire conveyences but without a lot of outside help taxi patrons may have to settle for riding around in beefed-up versions of standard assembly line products, whatever they may be. Whether the taxis of the current century will be more interesting than those of the last century remains to be seen.

Since Checker was the last American cab with jump seats, some cab companies with A8 Specials liked to advertise those extra seats by putting that information somewhere so everybody could see it, as the Chester Cab Company did when they emblazoned "Five Passengers" across the hood. The gentleman posing with this A8 Special was James Moynihan Basey who founded Cab Management Corporation in 1936. Cab Management, a large fleet owner, is headquartered in Long Island City and the Basey family is still involved with the company. The flame-shaped roof light was plastic and hailed from Checker's hometown of Kalamazoo, Michigan. They would adorn Checkers to the end in 1982. The headlight bezels on this car are incorrect. *Oldee Taxi Instruments*

Cab Management's James Basey points to a Rockwell meter installed in the rectangular hole that Checker Motors put in every model A8, A9, and A11 taxicab. Large enough for the major brands to fit in, the opening normally had an optional metal bracket to hold the heavy meters from underneath. The holes in the bracket matched the mounting receptacles of all postwar Rockwell meters. On the Checker A8, the glove box was a slide-out affair mounted under the dash. This was one of the few holdovers from the previous Model A6. *Oldee Taxi Instruments*

The front seat of the A8 Special was not a bad place to spend a 10-hour shift. The upholstery was the same textured vinyl used in the A6 and the floors were front and rear rubber matting unless the buyer specified Formica covering in the rear. The luggage rack over the passenger seat seems to be a final concession to the days of luggage up front. If somebody had to have a bucket seat, and a few fleets did, Checker would comply. *Ben Merkel*

The rear of an A8 Special looked like this. An optional privacy partition would pivot up and over the driver's head like a garage door. The optional Formica rear floor was tough but slippery when wet prompting Checker to install anti-slip tape on some later cabs so equipped. With the jump seats folded, there was unmatched legroom compared to its Detroit competitors. *Ben Merkel*

For a couple years, new and old taxis mixed while the transition to stock sedan cabs took place. For riders, it was a subtle change as sightings of the big DeSotos and fastback Checkers gradually became less and less. In New York City at that time, a taxi could stay on the road as long as it passed inspection so some stalwarts kept their old pre-1955 equipment on the road until the early 1960s. This view of Times Square circa 1956 confirms that a majority of the taxis were new A8 Checkers, Fords, Plymouths, or Dodges. Most of the big DeSotos pictured were now two or three years old, which meant that fleets would soon dump them. Like the A2 to A6 Checkers, the huge Skyviews were unwanted and regularly sold to boneyards for $25 apiece. *Nathan Willensky*

Since Checker Cab Manufacturing was a relatively small company, they looked at outside suppliers for major mechanical components. The engine was a Continental 226-ci six-cylinder flathead that was similar to, but not the same as, those used in other cars like Willys. Transmissions were Warner Gear products and much of the front suspension was lifted from the 1954 Ford. Checker made its own body stampings, interiors, and gas tanks right at the factory. The taillight bezels came from a 1954 Pontiac station wagon and when the cars were ordered with backup lights, 1953 Chevrolet bezels were employed. Headlight bezels were imported from the mid-1950s Willys Aero sedan. The A8 came in two styles, the six-passenger A8 Standard with a stick shift and manual driver's seat or the eight-passenger A8 Special that had a two-speed automatic transmission,

power brakes, power steering, and power driver's seat. For Checker fleet drivers used to the battlewagons of the recent past, it was a whole new world. This restored A8 Special is wearing Chicago Checker Cab markings, and is shown posing at the Checker factory recently. *Joe Fay*

When Plymouth knocked at Boston Checker Cab's door, the company almost always answered. The 1957 Plymouth had space age styling that made the cars built just 10 years earlier look really old. Boston Checker Cab's new taxi was a Plaza and it most likely had the venerable 230-ci flathead six with 132 horsepower. A little bit from cabs past was found in the old metal and glass roof light. The Hackney Carriage License for the City of Boston was on the grille. Whoever was in charge of striping these Plymouths with checkerboard at Boston Checker did a nice job on the hood treatment. *Oldee Taxi Instruments*

On a sunny day at Pier 88 in Manhattan circa 1959, an incredulous Checker A8 driver and a group of French Line dock workers observed the arrival of three Parisian taxis onto the streets of New York City. The license plates ended in a "75," which meant they operated in Paris. To the left was a Simca Aronde, the middle cab was a Peugeot 403, and the large cab on the right was a Simca Versailles. French rules required the meter to be mounted on a pole outside of the driver's window and that the cab number was presented outside on a metal holder at the lower right corner of the windshield. Owners frequently painted on the license plate numbers. *Nathan Willensky*

On March 19, 1959, hundreds of New York City taxis took part in a convoy to Albany to protest a 10-cent rate hike on all cab rides. This interesting scene, taken from the 167th Street exit on the Major Deegan Expressway in the Bronx, gives us a snapshot of the taxis in Manhattan at that time. The 1957 DeSoto Firesweep taxi is first in line and it shows us that old, familiar DeSoto was serving New York City again after a two-year hiatus. For fleet sales, it is thought that the flathead six and little else was installed in taxis. Regardless, DeSoto's cab-making days would end before the decade was out and the DeSoto nameplate itself would vanish shortly thereafter. In May 1959, only one 1959 DeSoto was operating as a licensed New York City taxi. Behind the first cab, in order, are these taxis: 1957 Dodge, 1958 Chevrolet, 1956 Dodge, 1956 Plymouth, two 1956 Dodges, Checker A8, 1957 DeSoto, 1958 Ford, another Checker A8, one more 1956 Dodge, and a 1957 Dodge. Note the similar plastic roof domes on all these cabs that read, "Taxi."

Ford was very aggressive in the New York City area and by 1958 was outselling everybody. A quick study of taxi brands and their total numbers in operation as of May 29, 1959 (all years): Ford 3,510, Checker 2,421, Dodge 1,889, Plymouth 1,856, Chevrolet 865, Studebaker 630, DeSoto 102, Pontiac 63, Chrysler 34, Rambler 24, Mercedes-Benz 12, Oldsmobile 11, Mercury 8, and Buick 7. These numbers flucuated every month as fleets phased in and phased out dozens of cabs at a sitting but it is remarkable that Ford went from being a nobody on Broadway to King of the Cabs in just a few years. The 1958 Fords with the taxi package came in mid-level Custom 300 trim and shared a

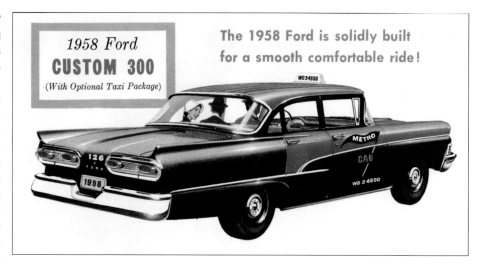

1958 Ford CUSTOM 300 (With Optional Taxi Package)

The 1958 Ford is solidly built for a smooth comfortable ride!

lot of parts with the police package. An Expanded Taxi Package offered all vinyl upholstery, rubber floor mats, grab handles, and pull straps. Ford offered three levels of heavy-duty equipment to suit the buyer. Standard power was a trusty overhead valve 223-ci six-cylinder engine that had been around since 1952. *Ben Merkel*

Chevrolet's 1958 offerings had taxis in two trim levels, the basic Delray Series and the intermediate Biscayne, which had a bit more exterior trim and a slightly different upholstery pattern in gunmetal and silver. Otherwise, the cabs were mechanically identical and most operators chose the 235-ci six motor combined with the optional Powerglide automatic. The three-speed column-mounted manual shifters were becoming less common in taxis because they were easy to abuse and the shifters themselves became troublesome with age. In cities like Chicago and New York, a cab was subjected to as many as 300 gear changes in a 12-hour period. Chevrolet advertised that the rear door hinges on its taxi packages would open 14 degrees more than regular models. The model shown is a Biscayne. *Ben Merkel*

Detective Frank Bartone from the Elizabeth, New Jersey, Police Department dusted this 1958 Plymouth Plaza cab for prints after it was used as a getaway car from a quadruple murder in New Brunswick, New Jersey. The cab was two years old and the paint was worn off the steering wheel from regular use. The passenger assist straps attached to the center posts were found in most taxi packages and Plymouth was no exception. Power was from a 132-hp flathead six but V-8 power was optional. The cabs were almost 205 inches long. The large bumper guards were well done and probably the work of a local aftermarket supplier. The license plate is notable for its odd size. *Nathan Willensky*

In the late 1950s, Studebaker-Packard was quietly selling taxis all over the place and had over 1,000 in New York City alone. The Econ-O-Milers were their own animal in that Studebaker took their largest body, which happened to be the 206-inch President, and did it up in their entry-level Scotsman trim to keep costs down. The headliner had a zipper for access to the roof light wiring. Motivation was from a 185-ci flathead six-cylinder engine that put out 101 horsepower. Production numbers for the Econ-O-Miler were approximately 1,118 units for 1958. From the looks of the roof light and the rates on the front doors, it is likely that this cab was heading for service in Manhattan. *Ben Merkel*

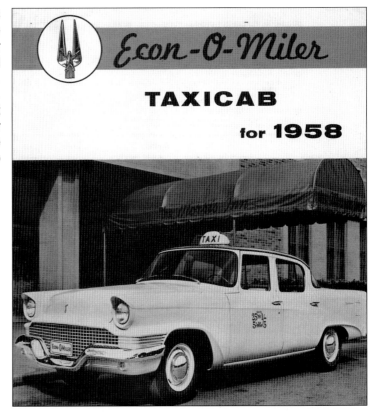

1958 Studebaker Economiler. *Ben Merkel*

EXTRA WIDE REAR DOORS allow for easy access and egress. Flat sill entrance is a safety-plus feature.

PLENTY OF LEGROOM for the tallest riders. Individual control rear dome lights and dual ash trays for passenger convenience.

A fairly flat rear floor was a plus for passengers. *Ben Merkel*

experienced taxicab operators prefer

Checker NOW, BETTER THAN EVER

MODEL A-9

Checker built the Model A9 taxi from October, 1958 until March, 1962 to the tune of about 20,000 units. A small portion of these were civilian Superba Model A10 sedans and wagons, introduced in 1960 to help replace sales lost by Checker's shrinking taxi market. These civilian models were the same as the taxis except for a few trim differences. The "Superba" name would eventually be replaced by the "Marathon" moniker, beginning in 1961. Private Checkers were frequently purchased by well heeled buyers looking for something different. To rake in their target audience, Checker Motors placed small ads in National Geographic magazine for years.

General Motors produced some of the most radically styled cars ever in 1959 and Chevrolet wasn't skipped over when the fins were given out. This 1959 Chevrolet Biscayne taxi worked for the Airport Cab Company in San Francisco and displayed an attractive two-tone paint job that matched the roof with the wheel rims. When a buyer ordered Chevrolet's Regular Production Option 330, they received a ton of heavy-duty taxi equipment in one comprehensive package that covered everything from all vinyl upholstery and wider opening rear door hinges to beefier mechanicals and special taxi carburetor. As with most cars built during this time, buyers could order a cab in 101 different ways and Chevrolet would build it for them. No factory-built 1959 Biscayne taxis have been spotted recently. *San Francisco Public Library*

Boston Checker Cab was looking for something in 1959 and, like other cities including Detroit, New York, Philadelphia, and San Francisco, they thought maybe an English Austin was the answer. It was not very large, could hold five-in-the-rear, and got 25 mpg with the 55-hp diesel engine. As cabbies found out, these English cabs were fine for around town but on high speed American-style airport runs, where seconds counted and big tips could be made, they topped out at around 60 mph. They weren't cheap to buy either with a price tag of $3,700 or almost twice the cost of a domestic gasoline fleet car. The theory was that they would last a long time and save $1,500 a year in operation and maintenance costs. To protect its investment in precious British metals, Boston Checker Cab gave this little Austin a professional grade bumper. As nifty as these cabs were, they never caught on with large fleet owners. Boston Checker Cab bought some Checker A9s around this time so perhaps this was a year of experimentation for them. *Oldee Taxi Instruments*

English Austins weren't the only foreign made diesels clattering around select American cities. San Francisco Yellow Cab put this 190D Mercedes Diesel into service on May 13, 1959, to see what it could do. Mercedes Diesels were and still are very popular taxis in all parts of the world but they couldn't seem to make a go of it in the States. High initial cost and expensive spare parts might have negated the fuel savings since gas was pretty cheap in those days. This cab still had the European turn signals on the front fenders. It's possible that the car was purchased in Germany and shipped to the US since Mercedes didn't import their taxi models into North America as a regular line. *San Francisco Public Library*

A New Yorker stepped out of a 1960 Ford Fairlane taxi and demonstrated how the chrome door handle was useful in exiting a modern cab. For the elderly, obese, or handicapped, new sedans from General Motors, Ford, and Chrysler weren't easy to get in and out of. When equipped with a partition, modest legroom became downright skimpy. Since Detroit sunk the floors into the frame to lower the rooflines, the transmission tunnel and doorsills became higher, creating problems for the less limber. Ford's Expanded Taxi Package included the chrome door handle on the right rear door, assist straps on the center doorposts, and full rubber flooring all around. Ford persisted with their 223-ci overhead valve six-cylinder motor and most cabbies ordered it. The plastic roof domes on both this 1960 Ford and the 1960 Ford and Chevrolet in the left lane are typical for this time period in Manhattan. The lack of a partition was a momentary phenomenon, as they would be back in a few years. No factory-built 1960 Ford Fairlane taxis are known to exist today. *Nathan Willensky*

Introducing the 1961 STUDEBAKER TAXI
The finest taxi available at any price

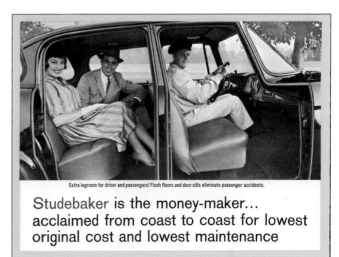

Extra legroom for driver and passengers! Flush floors and door-sills eliminate passenger accidents.

Studebaker is the money-maker... acclaimed from coast to coast for lowest original cost and lowest maintenance

The 1961 Studebaker Lark taxi may have been an older design but it was easier to get in and out of than many larger cabs due to its almost flat rear floor and flat doorsills. For the taxi operator on a tight budget, the Larks were a must see because they cost $2,252, were good on gas with the new 170-ci six, and Studebaker boasted that the Lark had the cheapest sheetmetal repairs in the business. As before, the Lark taxi was based on a decontented version of their biggest body so it was not a regular line sold to the public. Along with the usual heavy-duty taxi features found in the Lark, the 32-ounce vinyl upholstery was said to be flameproof. Approximately 1,108 of these heavy-duty sedans were built, most of them as taxis. Out of all the Lark cabs built, only two roadable examples, a 1962 and a 1963, are known to exist today. *Ben Merkel*

The compact Lark had enough room for two or three passengers in the rear and that's all a driver needed to make money. This particular operator seemed to be dressed more for a lab visit than a stint behind the wheel of a taxicab. *Ben Merkel*

Plymouth's taxis for 1961 featured some of the most unusual styling ever to come out of Chrysler Corporation and you either liked it or you didn't; there was not much middle ground. The other big news was under the hood where Mopar introduced its soon-to-be famous 225-ci slant six engine. The term "slant" referred to the 30-degree slant of the motor block to the right. Cabbies were pleased to find out that this new powerplant was good for a couple of hundred thousand miles with regular maintenance. It was so good that competitor Checker Motors tried to buy it and even went so far as to put a few slant six Checkers on the street. For one reason or another, the two wound up in court and Checker

went to Chevrolet power in 1964. The 1961 Plymouth Savoy taxi pictured most likely had the optional Torqueflite six transmission, an automatic advertised as being the only three-speed transmission developed for a six-cylinder taxi motor. Behind it lurked the new but unwanted Valiant taxi powered by a base 170-ci six. As of December 1960, only two Valiants were doing cab service in Kentucky. Ford and General Motors were having equally poor luck in the compact cab market. The problem was that operators couldn't make airport or hotel runs in a cab that couldn't handle a family of four with all of their luggage. No examples of either size Plymouth cab are known to exist today. *Ben Merkel*

Ford's new 1962 intermediate car, the Fairlane, was only 197 inches long and could reasonably handle three in back. Advertised as "hundreds less than the Fords that used to bear its name," it priced out near $2,900 with the 223-ci six and three-speed stick shift. Standard equipment included heavy-duty cloth seats in beige, green, or red, beefed-up springs and shocks, a larger clutch, and even steel speedometer gears. An Expanded Taxi Package installed rear arm rests, ashtrays in the front seatback, and rubber floor mats throughout. Beyond that, an Auxiliary Taxi Package generated roof light wiring, right rear door chrome handle, assist straps for the center doorposts, and a loose glove box in case the new owner wanted to install a meter. It is unknown how many were sold but none have been seen in a long time. *Ben Merkel*

FORD'S ALL-NEW '62 FAIRLANE TAXICAB

The First Taxi To Put Economy First

Even though Detroit was breathing down Studebaker's neck with two sizes of smaller taxis, the underdog car maker from South Bend, Indiana still managed to sell 1,772 Lark taxis in 1962, most with the 167 cubic inch, overhead valve six with 112 horsepower. Shown is the $2,760 1962 Lark DeLuxe taxi, built as before with the largest body in the Studebaker lineup wearing base level trim , a model not offered to the general public. 1963 wasn't a bad year with 1,121 Lark taxis coming out of the factory in Indiana but 1964 bombed out with only 450 produced. After decades of supplying the taxi industry with cars, Studebaker quietly ended cab production and there would be no more. *Nathan Willensky*

Dodge's 1964 Series 330 taxi was a popular fleet cab for all the right reasons. It was roomy with a huge trunk and, at a length of 209 inches, it wasn't too large on the outside. Compared to the 224-inch-long DeSoto battleships from 10 years earlier, the new Dodges were like speedboats. As was normal, most Series 330 taxis came with one of the most legendary powertrain combinations in cab history: the 225-ci slant six coupled with the optional Torqueflite automatic. After a couple years of creative styling from Chrysler, the 1964 Dodges became more mainstream. *Claude Lefebvre*

A fleet of 1964 Dodges Series 330 taxis sit on a lot in the New York City area. Judging from the men on the sidewalk holding signs, it was probably a strike situation. Having this many taxis sitting around a big city gathering dust was costing somebody some cash. *Nathan Willensky*

While Checker was the last cab in America with jump seats, it still wasn't good enough for them. In February 1964, using a formula that dates back a long time, Checker Motors came out with a slightly extended sedan that was nine inches longer in the rear door than their regular cab. Since there was more room in the rear now, two optional, rectangular jump seats brought the rear capacity up to six people. In its class it had no competition. The regular Checker taxi was a Model A11 and the long wheelbase version was called the Model A11E. Never made in large quantities, fleets of these modern jumbo cabs were rare. This 1973 Checker A11E has the same basic body of the 1964 A11E except that the front and rear windows were smaller on the older cars. Freshly decommissioned from the Fort Cab Company in Waynesville, Missouri, Old Number 16 was sold off in the late 1980s and presently is thought to reside in California. *Ben Merkel*

The interior of the Checker A11E was a throwback to the old pre-1955 Checkers and DeSotos with rectangular jump seats facing forward. The seats functioned but they were only comfortable for short trips, which was fine for a taxi. Everything was done up in tough, gray vinyl with rubber floor mats. *Ben Merkel*

With the jump seats folded, there was a ton of room in the Checker A11E. *Ben Merkel*

A pair of 1965 Checkers illustrates the variety of possible paint schemes that could have existed in New York City until 1968 when a new law made all medallion cabs yellow. If it were not for this law, Manhattan would have multicolored fleets like Chicago. Checker Model A11s, introduced in mid 1962, were little changed from the previous A9s except for a curved bumper and turn signals under the headlights instead of in the grille. Powering most Checkers this year was the 230-ci Chevrolet six with an optional 283 V-8. Transmission options included a Borg-Warner automatic or a three-speed manual transmission on the steering column or on the floor. Both of these cars are private Marathons turned into cabs since there are hardly any real 1965 Checker A11s left. It was normal for taxi companies to search out privately owned Checker Marathons to turn into taxis because they were essentially the same as an A11 cab except for trim differences like exterior chrome, carpeting, and different dashboard. *Chris Monier*

An increase in taxi robberies during the mid 1960s prompted driver complaints about safety. One proposed solution was to weld a locked cashbox to the floor and another involved bulletproof partitions. In 1965, Checker Motors came out with this bulletproof partition made of padded steel and bulletproof glass that was custom made for their own cabs. While the glass on the left was fixed, the window on the right went up and down and was vacuum controlled by a toggle switch under the dashboard. A pivoting cash drawer in the middle allowed money transfers without human contact. One way that Checker Motors tested partitions was to have employees bring their guns to work. *Ben Merkel*

The Checker taxi dashboard was full of old-fashioned tidbits like round gauges and metal knobs. The toggle switch for the partition was under the left part of the dashboard next to a panic button that made the top lights flash in the event of a holdup. These "bandit" lights were supposed to attract police attention. In those days, air conditioning was pretty rare in taxis but this Checker A11 had it. Unfortunately for the passenger, if they looked suspicous, the driver might close the divider window and keep all the cool air, or heat, up front. This was and still is a common complaint about partitions. *Ben Merkel*

Ford had a redesign in 1965 and offered their full-sized taxi models in the Custom or Custom 500 Series with the 240-ci six-cylinder motor as the engine of choice for most operators. The Expanded Taxi Package offered rubber flooring, pull straps, and a chrome handle on the right rear door, among other amenities. The 1965 Ford pictured is a Custom 500 made to look like a Chicago Checker Cab right down to the Checker factory roof light. Since Checker Motors owned Chicago Checker Cab, it is doubtful that they would own too many of a competitor's cabs. In New York City as of August 23, 1965, the following taxicab registration totals were reported: Dodge 6,746, Ford 2,920, Checker 1,229, Chevrolet 728, Plymouth 54, Studebaker 46, Chrysler 14, Mercury 4, Pontiac 4, Mercedes Benz 3, Rambler 2, Oldsmobile 2, and Buick 2. Of interest is that Ford had momentarily lost first place in Manhattan to Dodge and that no DeSotos of any year were left in service by this date. *Chris Monier*

While not nearly as popular as Chrysler's intermediate line, the 1965 Fairlane taxi found a few operators that appreciated its handy size and lower fuel bills. Statistically, the average cab ride involved 1.3 riders so it made no sense to some fleets to lug a nearly two-ton behemouth around for that 1.7 percent of riders needing four-passenger room. The 170-ci six-cylinder motor was a decent performer with 105 horsepower pulling 2,850 lbs around town. Allentown, Pennsylvania, Yellow Cab was the purported destination of this artists' rendering. The round, red objects on the trunklid could be cab company installed reflectors. *Chris Monier*

The 1968 Checker Model A11's profile was not unlike the 1967's profile except for one big difference: The windshield and rear window were a few inches taller. The small "dog dish" hubcaps were standard Model A11 issue unless a cabbie popped an extra $15.66 for full wheelcovers that, for 1968, were newly brought in from the Studebaker parts bin. The Checker Motors Corporation "CMC" was embossed in the center instead of the Studebaker "S". There wouldn't be any further glass size or full wheelcover changes until the end of production in 1982. The small hubcaps would remain standard until their disappearance around 1980.

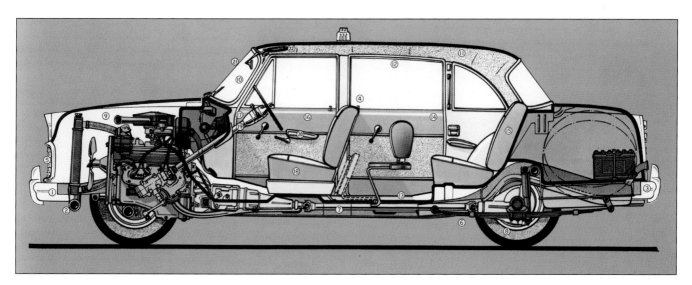

A cutaway of the 1968 Checker showed how the battery went in the trunk on most Checker taxis from this era. Between it and the spare tire, the trunk wasn't able to handle a lot of baggage. If the round jump seats were not in use, a lot of Checker patrons liked to carry their luggage with them where they could keep a tight grip on their valuables . Unlike most cars from the late 1960s, there were only a few inches between the grill and radiator.

The bucket seat wasn't dead yet. Checker Motors still offered one although it was almost always accompanied by a partition. As inviting as this seat might look in the picture, it wasn't terribly comfortable in real life. *Ben Merkel*

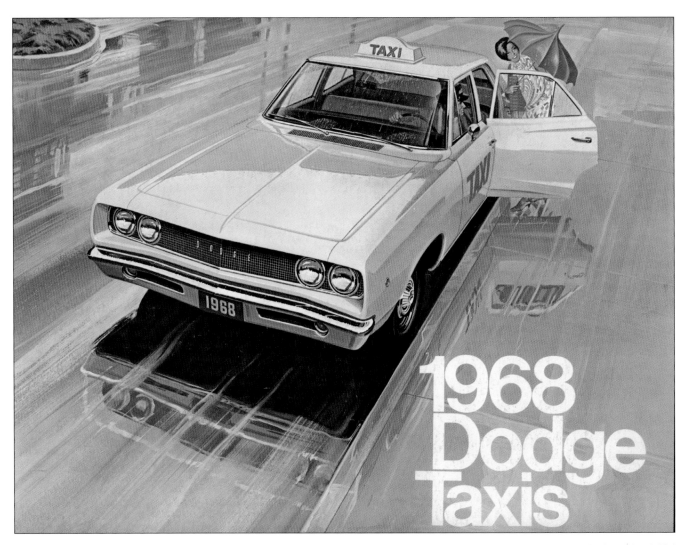

1968 Dodge Taxis

The Dodge Coronet and its twin, the Plymouth Satellite, continued their popularity streak in many American cities by combining a low initial purchase price with a mechanically durable six passenger, intermediate-sized cab with a generous warranty. They were aggressively promoted with offers such as, "Buy 10 Coronets and get the eleventh for free." Some large dealers took Chrysler's existing warranty and threw in another 25,000 miles to sink the hook deeper. A lot of cabbies and police departments couldn't get enough of these mid-sized Mopars. *Claude Lefebvre*

Dodge's largest taxi for 1969 was the Polara and, as this artists' rendering shows, it was available in any color including pink. Unlike the smaller Coronet, the Polara had a 230-hp, 318-ci V-8 as standard equipment with a Torqueflite automatic. With a length of 220.8 inches and a width of 79.3 inches, there was nothing diminutive about these 3,701-lb sedans and Dodge promoted the torsion bar front suspension and unibody contruction to operators. The trunks were gigantic. *Ben Merkel*

American Motors had a decent, intermediate sized Rebel "6" taxi for the cabbie that didn't have a lot of money to spend. The 232-ci six had 145 horsepower and was known for longevity. The taxi options list was long and included heavy-duty vinyl interior and door panels, front sway bar with stronger springs and shocks, a 55-amp alternator, and larger brakes. The cab was able to handle three in the rear seat and their luggage since the trunk was so roomy. *Ben Merkel*

AMERICAN MOTORS 1969

MONEY-SAVER...
OR
MONEY-MAKER?

TAXI

TAXI

REBEL "6" TAXICAB 4-DOOR

As a taxi operator, you're probably looking at the '69 Rebel primarily as a money-saver. Its modern-design, 7-main-bearing Six engine with 8 counter weights assures long trouble-free operation. The advance unit construction assures freedom from body squeaks and rattles. The extensive deep-dip rust-proofing treatments provide protection from rust and corrosion. That's all to the good.

But look at the Rebel as a money-maker. Passengers like its full 60-inch-wide rear shoulder room, comfortable coil spring seats. Drivers find its sharpest-of-all turning diameter, lean overall exterior dimensions a big asset in maneuvering to pick up a fare in tight quarters, quarterbacking its way through heavy traffic to drop that fare at his destination, and getting that flag up again for more business.

Take a moment to check Rebel's lower operating cost, higher gross specifications on the back page. If you were to design a taxi, yourself, from the ground up, chances are it would end up looking like a Rebel.

BUT DON'T BOTHER, WE'VE ALREADY DESIGNED THAT PERFECT TAXI FOR YOU!

The Checker Model A11, like all cabs, could be painted an almost endless variety of patterns and colors as was shown by this sharp looking 1970 with optional two-tone paint, spotlight, big hubcaps, factory installed roof light, and the "Checker Special" decals on the rear doors. Jump seats were optional on both wheelbases but not every fleet ordered them. Maybe half of the regular wheelbase A11s had jump seats but most of the longer A11E models did since leaving them off would have defeated the purpose of the bigger body. A 250-ci Chevrolet six coupled to a Borg-Warner automatic powered most A11 taxis since 1969 was the last year for a manual transmission in a Checker. *Ben Merkel*

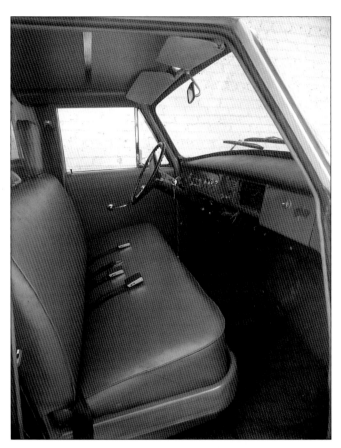

Before the federally mandated five-mph bumpers of 1973, several companies made water bumpers to replace the relatively ineffective stock bumpers installed by the taxicab manufacturers. These energy-absorbing bumpers used a series of water filled compartments with caps on top. Upon impact, the caps would blow off and the contents would shoot all over the place like a geyser dissipating the energy of the crash and protecting the taxi's sheetmetal. In cold climates an antifreeze mix had to be used to keep the bumpers from freezing solid. This water bumper is shown on a 1970 Checker but they were available for all the big brands. *Ben Merkel*

The dashboard of a 1970 A11 wasn't much different from the 1965 A11 except for a few changes made for safety's sake. Headrests, shoulder belts, a padded dashboard, and a Chevrolet steering wheel with an American Motors shift lever marked the most obvious differences. *Ben Merkel*

Ford's 1970 Custom taxi was almost devoid of trim and came with the excellent 240-ci six cylinder as the base motor. Almost everybody ordered them with automatic transmission, power steering, and brakes but this white example is an exception in that it's got the automatic but manual steering and brakes. On a big cab like this, Ford had a larger diameter steering wheel when power steering wasn't ordered. As usual, the base taxi and police packages were almost identical. This 1970 Ford Custom taxi was ordered for a taxi company in Binghamton, New York, and is the only one known to exist at this time. *Ben Merkel*

This 1970 Ford Custom has the Expanded Taxi Package, which included full rubber flooring, passenger assist straps on the center doorposts, and a chrome handle on the right rear door. The seats were reinforced with heavier springs for strenuous service. *Ben Merkel*

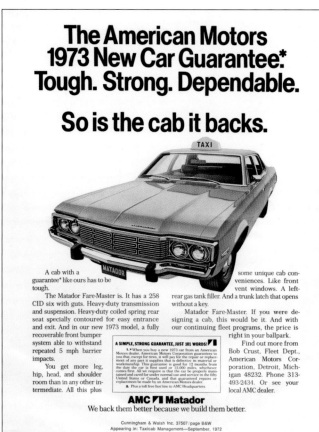

American Motors was heavily promoting their fleet business in the early 1970s and had contracts to supply Matadors and Ambassadors to police departments, taxi companies, and even to the US Military. To lure buyers into its 1973 Matador taxi, AMC offered a bumper-to-bumper warranty for 12,000 miles or 12 months on everything except tires. Today, this may not sound like much but back then it was a big deal. Standard equipment included the proven 258-ci six, which was married to an equally proven Chrysler Torqueflite automatic. Production numbers for the taxi are currently unknown but it was probably a fairly low number. None have been seen since the early 1980s. *Ben Merkel*

The old, bulletproof partition used by Checker since 1965 was updated around this time to a sliding window design that was much lighter by virtue of its aluminum construction and replacement of the thick, bulletproof glass with Lexan clear plastic. Checker would stick with this partition until the end of production in 1982. While these dividers worked well, they did rob the driver of legroom and caused annoying reflections at night. Checker's Model A11 had interiors colored in red, black, or two shades of gray. If a customer wanted a special seat material, they could send a roll of it to Checker and it would appear in their new car. *Ben Merkel*

Number 253, a Checker Cab Company Fresh-Aire Taxi, showed off its best desert pose wearing a National Taxicab Supply roof light. This 1973 Dodge Coronet cab probably had the 225 cubic inch slant six with optional automatic transmission and air conditioning which, by this time, was a common accessory on taxis operating in hot climates but wouldn't be mandated by law in some Midwestern and Eastern cities until the mid-1980s. Dodge sold a lot of base level Coronets to fleets in 1973 but it is unknown exactly how many of the 14,395 built were industrial strength taxis and police cars although guesses put it at around 3,500 units. The hand painted lettering on this Dodge was well executed and probably the work of one person, usually a local sign painter brought in for the day. To letter and number six new taxis could easily take a whole morning to accomplish and any door or fender repairs after that meant a repeat visit. The long standing practice of hand painted taxi lettering ended in the 1980s with the advent of computer generated pre-spaced vinyl lettering. Hand lettered cabs are so rare today that they practically qualify as mobile folk art. *Chris Monier*

With the gas crunches of the 1970s, many fleet owners turned to lighter, smaller taxis like the 1977 Dodge Aspen as a way to combat the gasoline blues. Their weight of approximately 3,345 lbs was a good 400 lbs lighter than most domestic large sedans and, when combined with the 225-ci slant six motor, they could generate 12 to 13 mpg around town versus the 9 or 10 mpg that the big cruisers got. For heavy-duty service, the police suspension was utilized along with heavy-duty wheel rims and the small cop hubcaps with the cooling holes. *Chris Monier*

Dodge had three sizes of taxi in 1977: the full-sized Monaco, the intermediate-sized Coronet, and the compact Aspen. Of the three, only the Monaco had a standard 318 V-8 engine; the other cabs still used a modern version of the 225-ci slant six introduced in 1961. Shown is the intermediate Coronet, a very popular taxi since it could carry three adults and had a decent trunk for a base fleet price of $3,499 with an additional $871.71 for the taxi package. *Chris Monier*

The mid-sized Plymouth Fury and its corporate twin, the Dodge Coronet, had the traditional taxi grab handles on the right rear doors and special seat bottoms that were beveled on the corners for easier entry and exit. *Ben Merkel*

A pink 1978 Chevrolet Impala seems very appropriate for Key West, Florida. The 9C6 taxi package included heavy-duty springs, brakes, and radiator and didn't share much mechanically with its civilian counterpart. These Impalas were among the last that didn't have computer-controlled engines. By 1980, a 229 V-6 would be the new standard powerplant and a computer-controlled carburetor arrived in 1981 along with the bane of all shop mechanics from now on, the dreaded "Check Engine" light. *Chris Monier*

A 1979 Chevrolet Impala with the 9C6 taxi package waited in the Chicago O'Hare Airport taxi pool in 1983. Equipped with the reliable 250-ci six cylinder as the standard powerplant, it was a popular car everywhere but in Chicago, where the two largest fleets, Yellow and Checker, still used Checkers, as did most of the other companies in town. The Impala is wearing the roof light off a Checker cab and so is the Chrysler Newport ahead of it. When cabs die or become too old, their roof lights are transferred to the new cabs along with meters, partitions, and anything else that is recyclable. *Ben Merkel*

Checker Motors was one of the few auto companies who could keep using the same basic sales brochures for years since their cars didn't change much. This 1979 Checker Model A11 ad shows a 1976 or 1977 Checker cab with the windshield wipers meeting in the middle. In 1978, this was changed to where they both went the same direction.

Checker Special decal- used from 1956 to 1982.

The late 1970s saw a movement asserting the rights of handicapped people to access public transportation and legislation came forth that not only dictated when vehicles were to be wheelchair accessible but also provided monies to explore ways of implementing it. One interesting project was this 1980 Oldsmobile Omega built by Minicars, Inc. of Santa Barbara, California. There were two built, one for the taxi show rounds and the other was leased for a nominal amount to several cab companies on a trial basis. It would hold one wheelchair or had fold-down seats for three persons. At least one of these Omegas still exists today. *Ben Merkel*

The original idea was for the operator to be able to open the right rear door and lower the ramp electrically from the driver's seat and then the wheelchair could be locked in via a lever up front. A rear shoulder belt pivoted out on an arm. The whole experiment was interesting except for two problems: A van could do the same job with less fuss and handicapped passengers didn't necessarily like riding around in a cab that looked like it was from Area 51. *Ben Merkel*

Vancouver Taxi in British Columbia operated a fleet of about 10 Checkers in the 1980s that had been adapted for wheelchair use, probably in Canada. The right rear door would open 180 degrees and a ramp would allow at least one wheelchair to enter. None are thought to exist today. *Paul Belanger*

In New York City you could usually tell a Checker fleet cab from an owner-operator unit by the striping and roof advertising. Fleet Checkers in Manhattan tended to have stripes on the roof and not on the sides because fleet cabs seemed to have more accidents, more often than private taxis. If you're constantly replacing fenders, stripes just cause problems. If they don't match, they look bad. If they're crooked, they look worse. The roof ads are another fleet cab tip off since advertisers prefer volume. Because roof ads are in the middle of the roof, the teardrop amber lights on the sides of the roof are turn signals as mandated by New York City law. Cabs without roof ads usually have the turn signals on the ends of the taxi light. This fleet Checker A11 was photographed in 1980 and is probably a 1979 or 1980 model. *Ben Merkel*

The lot next to the Checker showroom had dozens of mostly yellow New York City taxis for sale. Some had stripes on the top, some had stripes top and bottom. Others had air conditioning and tilt wheel some did not. Nearly all had the 229 Chevrolet V-6. Interestingly, the rate stickers were installed at the Checker factory and not at the dealer. Retail prices for a new 1980 Checker A11 began at $8,056 (dealer cost was $6,174) and anybody with a pulse and a wallet could have walked in off the street and purchased a new yellow Checker cab to take home and impress the neighbors. Few non-cabbies did that but many small town operators from surrounding states used to come to the big city and lay their money down for six or more Checkers at a time. *Tom Merkel*

The main Checker dealer near Manhattan was Checker Motors Sales Corporation at 35-30 38th Street in Long Island City, a location it had had since 1972. The showroom had black and white checkerboard flooring and the tile on the roof facade was taxi yellow. As the cabs parked in front demonstrated, this was the place to get parts and service because there were quite a few unique pieces on a Checker that were not to be found in the real world. Checker Motor Sales also handled much of the exporting business for the factory in Kalamazoo. *Ben Merkel*

Checker installed the 5.7 Oldsmobile diesel V-8 into their cars from 1979 to 1981 as a pricey $2,355 option designed to save fuel. Only 33 A11 diesels were built in 1980 and the following year approximately 90 left the building, most heading for New York City. The larger A11E diesels were rarer still with 13 built in 1980 and 7 built in 1981. While these diesel Checkers could double the city mileage of their gasoline counterparts, reliability problems made some owners convert them to gasoline-powered Oldsmobile 350s. The 1980 Checker A11 diesel shown was Number 11 in the Sumter, South Carolina, Yellow Cab fleet back in 1984. Number 11 had a partition and some nice hand lettering. A chrome script reading "Diesel" was normally installed on the left side of the trunklid. *Ben Merkel*

A row of new 1981 Checker A11s posed at City Cab in Binghamton, New York, after being purchased off the lot at Checker Motor Sales Corporation. They were basically New York City fleet cars, which means they had jump seats, frame and body reinforcements, rear window defogger, and stripes on the roof only. *Bob Hinkley*

Fritz Cajuste, medallion number 7A70, was one of the last Checker drivers in New York City and his ride, a 1981 Checker A11, was typical of an owner-operator vehicle. It had the stripes top and bottom, no partition, and he had replaced the stock Checker seat with one out of a luxury car. The "Checker Special" decals on the rear doors cost $13.50 for the pair. The silver trim along the fender openings was added by a body shop. Fritz Cajuste passed away in the late 1990s but his cab is still around. *Chris Monier*

The last big Chrysler Newport taxis were built in 1981 and even though they marked the end of truly large sedans at Chrysler, nobody really noticed. Rare when new, these Newport taxis were basically police cars with a 225 slant six-cylinder in place of a V-8. This 1981 Newport was part of the Chicago Checker Cab fleet and is shown in the cab pool at Chicago's O'Hare Airport in 1984. At this time, more than half of the cabs in Chicago were still Checkers. Note how the license plate matched the cab number. *Ben Merkel*

In February, 1982 these brand new orange Model A11 Norfolk, Virginia Yellow Cabs lined up just behind the Checker Motors factory in Kalamazoo, Michigan, awaiting shipment. They were ordered with top and bottom stripes at $45, $750 air conditioning, and tilt wheel at $127. The interiors were all black vinyl with the rear seat moved almost 10 inches forward to make room for more luggage space. This $79 option was called, appropriately enough, Rear Seat Forward, and it precluded the use of any jump seats. Other cities with a lot of Rear Seat Forward Checkers included Chicago, Illinois, and Lincoln, Nebraska. *Ben Merkel*

In 1988, the Norfolk Yellow Cab Company split their cab fleet between Checkers and Pontiac Bonnevilles. The Checkers ranged in age from 1979 to 1982 and were all phased out by 1989. Those that didn't sell were junked. A few survive today. *Ben Merkel*

Many of the last 1982 Checker A11 taxis had a $275 factory installed propane fuel option that only ran on LP gas. Three interconnected tanks held a maximum of 29 gallons and could go 200 to 300 miles on a full tank. The only engine available was the 229 Chevrolet V-6 six-cylinder hooked up to a Borg-Warner Century carburetor. Since they were alternative fuel vehicles, they didn't require computers, catalytic converters, or smog pumps. The trunk-mounted battery was relocated to the engine compartment and a lockable door took the place of the regular gasoline filler neck and cap. A chrome pressure release valve was mounted near the right rear roof post. This 1982 A11 with the factory propane option worked for Lincoln, Nebraska, Yellow Cab and is shown at the airport in 1984 with some silver paint flaking off of the taillight bezels revealing black primer underneath. This was a problem on later Checkers. The small license plate to the right of the main plate is a taxi license issued by the Nebraska Public Safety Commission. *Ben Merkel*

The dashboard of a 1982 Checker was not complex. An 85-mph speedometer, a fuel gauge, and a couple of chrome knobs borrowed from a mid-1950s Nash adorned it. To the lower left of the dash a square, chromed switch controlled the optional rear door locks. Illuminated rocker switches were regularly used to light up "Off Duty" roof lights or taxi domes to signal availability. Factory propanes had an "LPG primer" button to the right of the speedometer where the "Check Engine" light was placed on the gasoline jobs. *Ben Merkel*

The Freeport Taxi Company on Grand Bahama Island had one of the only major fleets in the world that used the long wheelbase Checker A11E models almost exclusively until the last pair was retired October 31, 1991. The two colors used, red or blue with a white top, were significant as the red color meant that duty had been paid on the vehicle and blue indicated that the cab was bonded and duty exempt. Checkers exported to the Bahamas were built without seat belts, headrests, or catalytic converters. Each day these cabs would go back and forth from the airport or cruise ship dock to Freeport, usually loaded to the hilt with tourists and their luggage, as this photo of a 1982 A11E shows. Rare when new, Checker only managed to produce about 82 of these in 1981 and a paltry 43 in 1982, their final year. Freeport Taxi bought 12 of the last batch, all blue and white. At least one still exists today. *Ben Merkel*

One of the few cab fleets in the US to have any 1982 long wheelbase Checkers was the Fort Cab Company of Waynesville, Missouri. Fort Cab serviced the Fort Leonard Wood military base for years until it lost the contract to do so around 1992. Out of approximately 40 Checkers in the fleet at the end, only two were 1982 A11E models that they had purchased from the original owners, the Fort Cab Company of Fort Knox, Kentucky. The hand-painted lettering was nicely done and is rarely seen today. Under the hood, there was only one choice, a 267 Chevrolet V-8 teamed to a GM Turbo 400 transmission. Retail price for a base A11E was $11,085 but options could push it to $13,000 without much trouble. United Parcel Service of Canada bought 14 brown 1982 A11Es and turned them into delivery cars with diamond metal plate interiors. At least eight of the last A11Es survive today. *Ben Merkel*

The late Felix Bucchioni, a longtime employee at Cleveland's United Garage, posed with the last Checker Zone Cab in town, a 1982 Model A11. Cleveland normally received six new Checkers every month, some yellow and some green. An oddity was the single, round jump seat ordered by Cleveland instead of the usual pair. When the last Checkers rolled off the truck, the switch was made to Chevrolet Impala taxis. *Ben Merkel*

With the Checker out of production, many operators turned to the Chevrolet Impala since it shared the same 229-ci V-6 as the defunct Model A11. While the Impala with the 9C6 taxi package didn't have the rear legroom of a Checker, it proved to be a workhorse. While functional, the square, staid body was jokingly referred to as having come from the "Three Box School of Design." Standard equipment in the taxi package included a heavy-duty frame, semi-metallic front brake pads, larger radiator, "door ajar" warning light, rubber floor mats, and heavy service front and rear seats in blue or tan. The Yellow Cab Company of Wheeling, West Virginia, bought Chevrolets to replace their Checkers and this 1983 Impala, Number 36, was photographed coming in off the street in 1987. Since some drivers preferred the relative safety of a partition, Number 36 had one. The intermediate-sized Malibu also came with a 9C6 package but it sold in far fewer numbers than the Impala. *Ben Merkel*

With Checker now gone, New Yorkers had to deal with mostly Caprices, Crown Victorias, and Dodge Diplomats. All were decent cabs but, when equipped with partitions as most were, there just wasn't adequate legroom. Traditionalists whined that first they lost their big DeSotos and now Checkers were disappearing. The Taxi and Limousine Commission of New York City approved this conversion of a 1984 Dodge Mini Ram Van to try to fill the rear legroom gap left by the old classic's departure. Built in Brecksville, Ohio, by Air Surrey, Inc., these taxis were called the Dispatcher series and came in two levels of trim. The Dispatcher pictured was the top of the line with a custom built body from the cowl back, featuring four doors and room for three comfortably behind a power partition. An additional Plexiglas divider separated the rear seat from the cargo area. The front bumper was extended about four inches but it wasn't terribly sturdy. *Ben Merkel*

With the cost of gasoline cresting at all-time highs, the idea of diesels was sounding better and better. Americans already had access to Peugeot 504 diesels so it made sense to put a few in Manhattan and let the chips fall where they may. Early 1980s 504 diesels were available in either the four-door sedan or station wagon form. Most didn't last more than a couple of years but a few stayed on the road until the late 1990s. Some used examples were sold to City Cab of Binghamton, New York, for further use. Considering New York City's early experiences with French taxis in 1907, a diesel experiment seemed a fitting reason to audition on Broadway again. None are thought to exist today. *Frédéric Robert*

As long as there were experimental French cabs running around Manhattan, the Swedes decided to field some of their own products in an attempt to cash in on the large New York City cab market. To test the waters, a modest fleet of early 1980s Volvo 244 taxis was painted yellow and put into rough service. As the ad showed, Volvo was pretty proud of their taxi candidates. Like most of the experimental fleet cabs before them, the Volvos were seen for a few years and then they quietly vanished. Some Model 244s were used as cabs in other parts of the country but they never caught on in a big way despite the fact that the 244 had a reputation for being one of Volvo's best cars. *Frédéric Robert*

A row of brand new 1988 Chevrolet Caprices was getting hacked up in the Cleveland Yellow Cab garage. While they have been striped and decaled for duty, the Chevrolet price stickers were still on the rear windows. The fuel-injected 4.3-liter V-6 was a durable motor and, when combined with a boxy sedan that was easy to work on and to see out of, these square Caprices with the 9C6 taxi packages were very popular with cab operators. Full-sized Chevrolets of this vintage are still used as "for hire" vehicles in the US and abroad. *Ben Merkel*

Ford's 1988 Crown Victoria LTD "S" taxi was powered by a fuel-injected 302-ci V-8 that put out 160 horsepower through an automatic overdrive transmission. The standard "S" fleet car with the taxi package included a 3.08:1 rear axle ratio, heavy-duty frame, taxi suspension, and low gear lockout on the transmission to prevent the driver from winding out the motor by manually holding the transmission in low gear under hard acceleration. A New York City Package deleted the right coat hook, substituted a diagonal door handle in place of the standard door pull handle, and provided extra wiring so the customer could install the roof-mounted turn signals as required by law. In New York City during the late 1980s, Chevrolet was the King of the Cabs with 88.6 percent of the Manhattan market and Ford was hanging in there at roughly 10.2 percent. The victory was not to last, as Ford would take the crown back after GM made the Caprice disappear in 1996. *Ben Merkel*

In 1988, Buckeye Auto Wrecking near Columbus, Ohio, answered an old taxi riddle: How can you park 71 Checkers and one Chevrolet in 36 spaces? *Ben Merkel*

When the 1991 redesigned Chevrolet Caprice 9C6 taxis came out, the styling polarized cabbies. Compared to the "three-box" Caprices before them, these were a radical departure for Chevrolet even though the chassis remained fairly static. Powering this new arrival was a 305 V-8, which wasn't very popular with cab companies who would rather have had a six. Chevrolet heard their pleas and installed the 4.3-liter V-6 into the 1992 Caprice. Cleveland's United Garage wouldn't order any 1991 models with the 305 so they waited for the 1992 models to show up as this picture portrays. Soon these bare yellow cabs would wear stripes, door logos, roof lights, and meters installed at the taxi garage. *Ben Merkel*

By 1992, Columbus, Ohio, tied with Waynesville, Missouri, for being one of the last places with a lot of Checkers. In 1981, Columbus' United Transportation ordered over 200 Model A11s under the Yellow, Hills, and Radio Cab banners. When most other cab companies were getting out of Checkers in the mid 1980s, United refurbished their A11 fleet and ran them up to 700,000 miles and more before final retirement. At least 10 still exist today. *Ben Merkel*

A freshly hacked up 1992 fleet Caprice showed off its new stripes, door logos, and roof lights at Cleveland Zone Cab. Soon, it would be ready to carry its first customer. To make the company's "bullseye" logo fit the Caprice door, somebody had to slice off the very bottom of the circle where it hit the lower door moulding. Since the late 1980s, the City of Cleveland has restricted cab ages to five years from the date that the taxi is put into service, not according to the year of the cab. *Ben Merkel*

Kennedy Airport near New York City has a large cab pool where taxis wait, sometimes for hours, to go into the airport with the hopes of scoring a lucrative run to the suburbs. In 1993, the older Caprices like the 1990 model in the foreground were being slowly replaced by the new design, nicknamed "Shamu" in some circles, after the famous Sea World whale. The only other kind of cab sharing the lot with Chevrolet was old buddy, Ford. The two had been battling for Manhattan since the mid-1950s. With the demise of the Dodge Diplomat and Plymouth Gran Fury line in 1989, Chrysler's long taxi presence in Manhattan quietly ended. The round, orange lights on the trunklids are bandit lights that flash to alert law enforcement to a cab robbery in progress. Another one is found on the front. *Ben Merkel*

When the Fort Cab Company of Waynesville, Missouri, lost their contract to service the military base around 1993, suddenly about 40 Checkers were out of work, put up for sale, and were stored on this lot close to the base. Coca Cola bought most of the fleet and turned them into green Surge cars. Surge was a popular soft drink and the cars were given away as prizes in the mid-1990s. At one time, Fort Cab used to give the military decommissioned Checkers to blow up for target practice. *Ben Merkel*

Surge cars looked like this and sported redone interiors with large music radios built into each dashboard. Most of them are still around today. *Chris Monier*

The last fleet Caprices were built this year and a lot of police departments and taxi companies were incredulous that there was no longer a full sized, rear drive, heavy-duty Chevy sedan to order. As a stopgap measure, some panicky fleets ordered a bunch at the end and put them into service slowly. The 4.3-liter V-6 was replaced in 1994 by a 200-hp, 4.3-liter V-8, which was basically a detuned Corvette engine. Since taxi fleet owners tend to equate high horsepower with poor fuel economy and increased accident rates, the optional 260-hp 5.7-liter V-8 was probably only ordered by police departments making undercover taxis. Interior choices were cloth or vinyl in blue or tan with a heavy-duty seat option. An aftermarket sliding partition for a Caprice was about $325. This 1996 Caprice was Number 27 in the Ann Arbor, Michigan, Yellow Cab fleet circa 2001. *Ben Merkel*

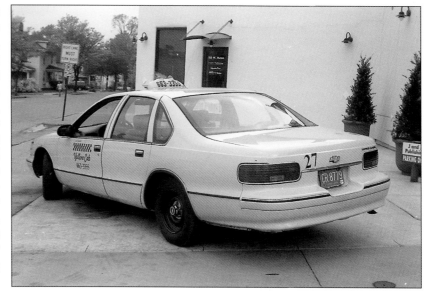

With the Caprice now gone, the Ford Crown Victoria became the last rear-wheel-drive, heavy-duty sedan left for cabbies to order. Under the hood, a 4.6-liter V-8 with 200 horsepower was channeled through a four-speed automatic transmission. Anaheim Yellow Cab near Los Angeles operates a fleet of Crown Victorias built from Ford to run on compressed natural gas or CNG. Dependability, low cost fuel, and low emissions were the big selling points for these alternative fuel taxis. Ford began selling CNG fleet cars beginning in 1999 but discontinued the program around 2004. New York City also used CNG Crown Victorias and even went so far as to give the CNG cabs extra time to stay in service beyond their gasoline counterparts. *Chris Monier*

On November 28, 2001, Ford introduced a slightly stretched Crown Victoria taxi using their existing Lincoln Town Car stretch as a base. The extra six inches provided paying customers with 7.7 extra cubic feet of room, which helped a lot in cabs with partitions. The concept sprang from Mayor Rudy Giuliani's quest for a roomier taxicab and the project involved the Ford Motor Company working with New York City's Taxi and Limousine Commission. A majority of the first cars went to Manhattan at a cost of $25,890 apiece. For an additional $785, an option package included air-conditioning outlets in the rear compartment. The front push bar was an aftermarket item usually installed by a meter shop. These Crown Victorias were the first custom built Ford taxis since the 1930s. *Chris Monier*

On February 22, 2005, San Francisco Yellow Cab purchased ten 2005 Ford Escape Hybrid SUV taxis and was the first to use hybrid sport utility vehicles as taxis. The Escapes, powered by gasoline and/or electricity, proved popular with their new owners. San Francisco Yellow Cab declared that their fuel economy was far better than other cabs in the fleet and the EPA noted that tailpipe emissions were down 97 percent from current standards in the hydrocarbon and nitrogen areas. *San Francisco Yellow Cabs*

Since Manhattan has a lot of taxis packed into a relatively small area, it makes sense that it would be a good place to test a low polluting vehicle,, and on November 10, 2005, some two-wheel-drive Ford Escape Hybrid SUVs went into service there. Initial results were promising: 36 mpg in city driving resulted in almost a 500-mile cruising range. According to the New York City Taxi and Limousine Commission, since each taxi in the city can average 100,000 miles per year, the fuel savings could pay for the hybrid's additional cost within a year. It is ironic that, after 100 years of evolution, American taxis are becoming more eco-friendly like their 1897 Electrobat ancestors. *Ford Motor Company*

Taxi Hats

Since the first taxis appeared on the streets of New York at the end of the Nineteenth Century, cabbies always wore head gear. Beginning in 1897 with the fancy top hats worn by the first Electrobat drivers, regular conductor style hats became popular when drivers began to sit inside the cab.

A distinctive sign for chauffeurs and hotel bellmen, the cap became a well-recognized feature among cabbies. Elegance, service and courtesy were represented by taxi drivers at that time and the hats became a symbol cab companies used to promote these qualities to the public.

Most of the time, a badge or a name script was placed above the visor: Yellow Cab, Checker, Black and White were just a few of the endless company names that could be found on a cap.

Yellow Cab hat, circa 1930.

In the late 1930s, conductor style caps changed to more of a service station attendant style. There are literally hundreds of different taxi hat styles. Among them, a very well known and fine example is the Yellow Cab hat.

A Kansas City Gelhaar make Yellow Cab hat, circa 1940.

Conductor-style Yellow Cab hat, circa 1920.

Checker Cab Co. hat (Chicago, circa 1960).

As Red Skelton shows in the 1950 movie *The Yellow Cab Man*, taxi drivers in those days almost always wore a hat. While it isn't true anymore, there was a time when a jacket, tie and a yellow hat were common cabbie attire.

Lancaster Uniform Cap Co., Inc.
Maker of the Famous Yellow Cab Hat

The Lancaster Uniform Cap Co., Inc. was started in 1929 in Detroit, Michigan as FIGMOR CAP by Meyer Figoten and his son Maurice. It was relocated to Los Angeles, California, in 1945.

Many headwear related items were made, such as "bee keeper" helmets, California Highway Patrol motorcycle soft caps (before helmets), uniform headwear during World War II for the Army Air Corps, the Marine Corps, and the U.S. Navy. The company still makes these for veterans that need replicas or need their old caps refurbished.

Over the years, the company bought out three or four other cap manufacturers in Los Angeles. Eventually the company name was changed to the brand name they had always used: Lancaster.

As can be seen by the original logo at right, the name didn't come from a U.S. city or town but from the horsemen that were part of the Lancaster Guard, serving the Queen of England. During that time, Carl Figoten, the son of Meyer & Chairman of the Board, took full control of the company and this is when Lancaster started specializing in Uniform Headwear and Veteran's Caps.

In 1975 Lancaster moved to a building at 680 South Imperial St. in Los Angeles from 4th and San Pedro, also in Los Angeles.

In 1982, Ernest Aguila, the current CEO, started with Lancaster and brought along his wife Martha (Corp Secretary) to run the bookkeeping and office operations. Ernest also started the trend towards automation; to de-skill operations, increase productivity, and maintain quality.

His knowledge in automated industrial sewing machines, repairs, electronic components, computer programming, engineering and digitizing transformed Lancaster Uniform Cap Co., Inc. into a vibrant, state of the art manufacturer.

Elizabeth Anne Aguilar/DeWeese, daughter of Ernest & Martha, currently works as the Assistant Office Manager, and Ernest Anthony Aguilar, son of Ernest & Martha, currently holds the position of Production Manager. Carl Figoten passed away on November 4, 2001. Ernest Aguilar Sr. is President/CEO and Chairman of the Board.

On September 1, 2004 Lancaster moved to a new location, 5522 Olive Street, Montclair, CA 91763, a brand new building located approximately 30 miles east of downtown Los Angeles, 6 miles away from Ontario, California, Airport.

Lancaster Uniform Cap Co., Inc. remains the only cap manufacturer west of the Mississippi.

Old Lancaster ad published in *Taxicab Industry, Auto Rental News* (June 1959).

Vintage Lancaster 1950 Yellow Cab hat. Note the real open cane head band for better ventilation on hot days.

Another Lancaster driver hat from the Red Cab co. (late 1950s).

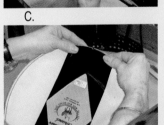

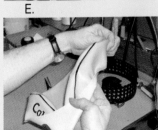

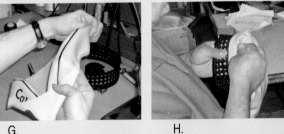

A.

B.

C.

D.

E.

F.

G.

H.

I.

J.

This Lancaster Checker Cab hat has the optional Checkerboard headband, which could be removed during the summertime.

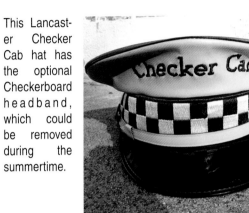

A 1967 Lancaster Driver hat from Long Beach, California.

A. Embroidery on panels ready to be cut.
B. Sewing real cane frame together preparing for the cover.
C. Checking sides to finish frame for correct sizing of side seams.
D. Sweat protector with Lancaster logo being prepared.
E. Sweat protector being sewn onto the cover top.
F. Sewing the sides of the cover to the top of the cover.
G. Turning the cover inside out for final sewing inspection before mounting to the frame.
H. After cover is sewn to frame, one more inspection.
I. The visor being inspected in preparation for mounting to the frame.
J. The visor being sewn to the cap.

Circa 1940 Taxi driver cloth hat with winged badge.

Oval-shaped 1945 Radio Cab hat badge.

Octagon-shaped 1964 taxi driver badge from Royal Oak, Michigan.

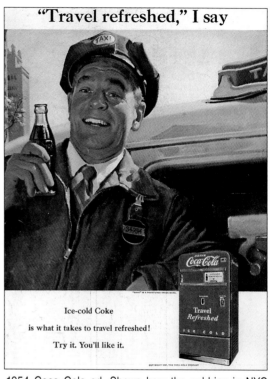

"Travel refreshed," I say

Ice-cold Coke

is what it takes to travel refreshed!

Try it. You'll like it.

Travel Refreshed

1954 Coca Cola ad. Shows how the cabbies in NYC wore their hack driver badge suspended to their jacket collar. Notice the cloth driver cap and the J. Waters rooflight on the taxi.

New York City Hack Driver Badges

From 1909 to the early 1950s, every taxi driver in New York had to wear his Hack driver badge on himself. It could be placed on his hat or on his jacket. The badge had a different shape every year. Here are some fine examples of those vintage badges.

1923 Public hack driver badge with its leather holder.

1909 hack license.

1916 hack driver license.

1925 Public hack driver badge.

1926 Public hack driver badge.

1927 Public hack driver badge.

1933 Public hack driver badge.

1937 Public hack driver badge.

1938 Public hack driver badge.

1928 Yellow Cab badge.

1937 winged Yellow Cab badge.

1937 winged Black and White cab badge.

1948 winged Yellow Cab badge.

1946 Los Angeles Yellow Cab badge.

1981-'83 taxi driver license, Buffalo, New York.

Cloth emblems from National Taxicab Supply, circa 1950.

NATIONAL TAXICAB SUPPLY COMPANY

This photo was taken in July of 2005. Rooflights on shelves are ready to be packed and shipped out to cab companies everywhere.

National Taxicab Supply Co. has been the largest source of taxicab equipment in the U.S. since 1946. Its founder, Max Heim, having been a former cab driver, returned home from WWII and found it difficult to locate a central source of taxicab supplies. Some companies manufactured rooflights and others made meters. There was, however, no single company that offered a variety of equipment.

At its location in San Francisco, National Taxicab Supply Co. manufacturers rooflights, printed forms, advertising carriers and decals, including checkerboard stripes. In addition, it is a distributor for Centrodyne and Pulsar Taximeters, the two largest taximeter companies in the US. On a local level, the company does installations of all its products as well as radios and cameras.

Back in the 1960s, National Taxicab Supply was also the largest authorized distributor of all electric Viking meters and carried a wide variety of taxicab equipment such as: Dispatch sheets, waybills, scriptbooks, cloth emblems, Brite-lite and Colvin Rooflights, coin changers, gear boxes cables and taxi stand signs.

The current owner, Linda Danzig, began working for the company in 1970. She purchased it in 1982 and continues to oversee its operations.

Customers can order on-line, through the mail or by telephone. The company ships its products throughout the U.S. and Canada, as well as other countries, on a daily basis.

This photo was taken Nov 27, 1956. Little has changed since then. Plastic rooflights are ready to be heat pressed. Some are cooling off on the shelves, before receiving lettering and tattletales, while others are ready to be shipped out.

An employee at National Taxicab Supply supervises the heating process of turning a flat piece of Plexiglass into an attractive, streamlined rooflight. Hardly anything has changed since the 1950s and the same old press is still on the job. In the background, the bright colored lights are waiting to be assembled.

The old wooden pieces, shaped after the different light styles, are still in use.

BRITE-LITE Rooflight model E-3. 18 in. long x 6 in. high x 8 in. wide.

BRITE-LITE Rooflight model G-6. 18 in. long x 7 in. high x 8 in. wide.

COLVIN rooflight model No.7 with large curved face and flat rear. 19 in. long x 5 in. high x 6 in.wide.

COLVIN rooflight model No. 7. 19 in. long x 5 in. high x 6 in.wide. Easy four-screw installation.

COLVIN rooflight model No. 4. 24 in. long x 5 in. high x 6 in. wide, mounted on a rubber cushion to fit the contour of the modern car tops.

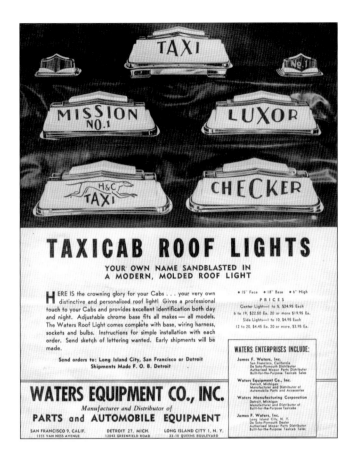

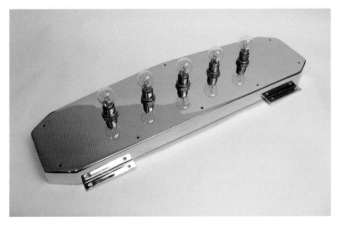

Here is a fine example of a Waters rooflight. The word "Skyline" is etched into the glass dome. Because they were made in larger quantities, the "Yellow" light had the more ornate, embossed letters. The base, under the roof, held the light bulbs and electric wires. There were 5 holes drilled into the roof of every DeSoto Skyview cab to fit the five light bulbs.

One of the most interesting advertising rooflights ever to be produced was this incredible one used by a cigarette manufacturer back in the 1980s. Two torsos, a woman and a man, appeared to be coming out of the roof of the cab, holding a cigarette in their hands. The cigarette brand, Benson and Hedges, was advertised on both sides of the roof sign. Some people thought that actors were paid to stand out of the roof! Made of resin, this advertising roof promotion was used at least in New York City. With the emergence of anti-tobacco laws, signs like this one became extinct pretty fast.

Taxi rooflight model "Buffalo" from American Cab-lites. The most expensive light in the 1955 catalog was priced at $47.50. A single lightbulb inside the head made the red eyes light up. A few of those lights are known to survive.

Circa 1955 Taxi Rooflight model "Wheeling," from American Cab-lites—14 inches high! Talk about aerodynamics!

Surviving example of an old Identity rooflight, circa 1930. The name of the company was applied on the white cylinder and the phone number painted underneath. The same light can be seen, new, advertised in the photo on the right.

Identity rooflights on a trade show display. The sign reads: "Can be seen from both front & rear." The first rooflights were built in above the windshield and could only being seen from the front.

Model C-35 from American Cab-lites. A product of Cabometer, Inc. (Anniston, Alabama). The word "Yellow" is made of cut-up black plexiglass letters glued to the yellow dome.

Typical 1970s rooflight from New York City. Made of cast aluminium. The light usually said "TAXI" on both sides until the late 1970s, when it changed to the medallion number. This one has the optional second story, which normally read "On Radio Call."

On a taxi the most noticeable feature, besides the bright colored scheme, is without a doubt its rooflight.

Placed on the highest point on the roof, its size, shape, color and specifications changed radically from the early years to now.

The first cabs had small rooflights built into the roof line above the windshield. When cars got all-steel tops, signage was moved to the middle of the roof so it could be seen from the front and from the rear.

The rooflight sizes reached a peak around 1940 with amazing big lights found on DeSoto and Packard taxicabs.

Through the years, many different materials were used to make them: early ones were made of thick glass, enamel, heavy cast iron, aluminium, plexiglass, and later, plastic.

BRITE-LITE rooflight model P-8, from National Taxicab Supply. The suggested lettering for the rear was the company name, cab number or phone number.

One of the latest rooflight styles for New York City (1992-2005). Made of plastic, it is lighter than the old lights from the 1970s.

Circa 1958 the typical Manhattan rooflight was white with red plastic. These three photos show every angle of that nice looking light.

Checker rooflight from 1939, a heavy sign made of glass and cast iron base. With amber lights on each side it was a real piece of art like the Waters light.

Checker factory rooflight. Also known as the "flame" type, was factory issued as an option on every Checker cab from 1948 to 1982. Color and lettering could be adjusted to any cab company's needs. They were made by a local company in Kalamazoo, Michigan.

1955 Quick Cab rooflight from American Cab-lites, model "Chester." Size 17 in., base 8 in. high.

Typical Taxi rooflight from Washington DC. 8 inches long. Note the black, plastic band that runs along the top. Used since the 1980s.

Airport rooflight from Plasticraft, a Washington state based company. In production from perhaps 1960 until recently. Note how the aircraft was inverted to fit on the sign.

Taxi License Plates

Many states have license plates with either the word "taxi" right on them or a series of letters or numbers reserved for taxis only. Some cities or public safety commissions also issued their own, smaller taxi plates in addition to a large plate. Every color of the rainbow can be found on taxi plates and here are just a few examples.

1977 taxi state plate from Connecticut.

1987 taxi city plate from New York City.

1979 taxi city plate from Buffalo, New York.

1977 taxi city plate from Waukesha, Wisconsin.

1969 taxi state plate from Nebraska.

1972 taxi city plate from Denver, Colorado.

Aldee, from Oldee Taxi Instruments in Long Island City, New York, is "hacking up" a new taxicab by preparing the rooflight for mounting.

Carlos Pampin, from Oldee Taxi Instruments, is fixing an electrical problem on a New York City rooflight.

Compufare digital electronic meter from the late 1970s. Made in Waltham, Massachussetts, this meter was issued just before the LCD meters. Fare numbers would light up on those four round glass cylinders.

A meter shop is a specialized garage for taxicabs, where many services can be performed, including a complete "hack up" featuring a full yellow paint job, installation of a taximeter, rooflight, medallion, rate stickers, robbery light, heavy duty bumper guards and a partition between the driver and passengers. Regular work includes maintenance, inspection, and calibration of the meters. Records of all repairs have to be transmitted to the authorities.

Oldee Taxi Instruments is a typical New York meter shop. Owned by the Gallego family, their shop is situated on Vernon Blvd. in Long Island City and was created in 1975.

Alvaro, a.k.a. "Aldee," knows the taxi business, as he drove a cab in the 1970s prior to being offered the management of a small taxi meter shop because of his electronic and mechanical expertise. Three years later, after an intensive training in Stockholm (for Swedish HALDA meters), he became independent.

A meter shop is regularly inspected by the New York TLC (Taxi and Limousine Commission) for the safety and protection of the passengers and requires qualified technicians, programmers, and electricians to keep modern cabs on the road.

Aldee is also a long time taxi lover and has an extensive collection of old taximeters, vintage taxis and memorabilia. He regularly supplies props for movies and outfits taxis for all types of commercials, television and movie productions.

1925 Ohmer meter, model H. One of the early meters with printed receipt. Ohmer was a major player among taximeters manufacturers from 1915 to the mid-1950s.

Viking electro-meter, manufactured in Belleville, New Jersey (widely used in the country from 1960 to 1980).

1968 Argomatic taximeter, also called a "Hot seat" meter, was part of an experiment in NYC. This meter was automatically activated when the passenger sat on the rear seat. This system would prevent dishonest taxi drivers from "forgetting" to turn on the meter.

1984 Halda Model M8. This electromechanical, Swedish made meter was used widely in the U.S. and all around the world and is perhaps the most well known meter of all time.

George Probs, an employee of Cab Management Corporation in Queens, New York, stands in front of the taxi garage holding a Metrometer ready to be installed in a Ford Crown Victoria taxi.

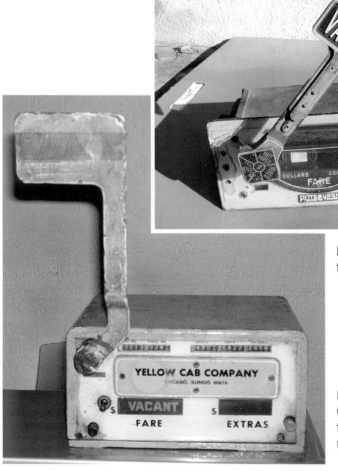

Beautiful Pittsburgh meter from the late 1960s.

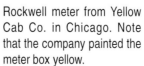

Rockwell meter from Yellow Cab Co. in Chicago. Note that the company painted the meter box yellow.

THE ARGO T-12 TAXIMETER

COLLECTS EVERY POSSIBLE NICKEL OR DIME OF INCOME

Here are some of the stickers you can find inside a New York City cab. They help drivers warn passengers about what they should and shouldn't do in a cab.

Current door sticker for the Cleveland Yellow Cab Company. The same bullseye design has been used since the 1960s.

Official City of Los Angeles taxicab seal—any cab without the seal is a bandit cab with no legal authorization to operate in the city. The building in the background is the Department of Transportation building on Main street. The taxi license number appears on the sticker situated on the front doors.

"Radio dispatched" logo displayed on the front doors of Morton Cab Company taxis in Cicero, Illinois, circa 1988.

Chicago's Checker Taxi Company logo. This sticker was found on the rear doors of the cabs until recently. Checker Motors Corp. owned both Checker Taxi and Yellow Cab Co. in Chicago.

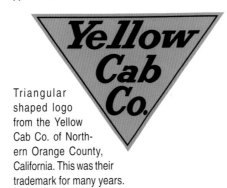

Triangular shaped logo from the Yellow Cab Co. of Northern Orange County, California. This was their trademark for many years.

National Transportation logo. The largest cab company in NYC during the mid-1950s. In 1952, they operated more than 1,600 Checker cabs on the streets of New York.

NEW YORK taxi fares since 1952

Date of Fare incr.	Initial charge	Charge per Add'l mile	Charge for Wait time	Charge per: Mile	Minute	Avg Fare
before 1952	$0.20 first 1/4 mile	$0.05 per 1/4	$0.05 per 2 min.	$0.20	$0.025	$0.81
July 1952	$0.25 first 1/5 mile	$0.05 per 1/5	$0.05 per 90 sec.	$0.25	$0.033	$1.03
Dec. 1964	$0.35 first 1/5 mile	$0.05 per 1/5	$0.05 per 90 sec.	$0.25	$0.033	$1.13
jan. 1968	$0.45 first 1/6 mile	$0.10 per 1/3	$0.10 per 2 min.	$0.30	$0.05	$1.45
Mar 1971	$0.60 first 1/5 mile	$0.10 per 1/5	$0.10 per 72 sec.	$0.50	$0.08	$2.25
Nov. 1974	$0.65 first 1/6 mile	$0.10 per 1/6	$0.10 per 60 sec.	$0.60	$0.10	$2.64
Mar. 1977	$0.75 first 1/7 mile	$0.10 per 1/7	$0.10 per 60 sec.	$0.70	$0.10	$3.01
July 1979	$0.90 first 1/7 mile	$0.10 per 1/7	$0.10 per 60 sec.	$0.70	$0.10	$3.16
Apr. 1980	$1.00 first 1/9 mile	$0.10 per 1/9	$0.10 per 45 sec.	$0.90	$0.13	$3.96
July 1984	$1.10 first 1/9 mile	$0.10 per 1/9	$0.10 per 45 sec.	$0.90	$0.13	$4.06
May 1987	$1.15 first 1/8 mile	$0.15 per 1/8	$0.15 per 60 sec.	$1.20	$0.15	$4.93
Jan. 1990	$1.50 first 1/5 mile	$0.25 per 1/5	$0.25 per 75 sec.	$1.25	$0.20	$5.57

July 1952, New York City, a very busy summer day at the taxi garage! The rates changed from 20 cents the first 4th of a mile to 25 cents the first 5th of a mile! This employee applied the new number "5" decals over the obsolete numbers, then rolled them for perfect adhesion.

Rates before 1952. Typical lettering for New York City.

Back in May 1987 The Statue of Liberty was chosen to appear in the background of the new rate stickers.

One buck for the first 1/9th of the mile was reached in April 1980. The additional night charge was on a separate sticker as not all cabs were operating at night.

The two dollars initial charge was proposed in 1997 on a new rate sticker with darker yellow color.

Checkerboard Stickers

Did you ever wonder what checkerboard stripes on a Checker cab were made of? Imagine a fleet of 1,200 Checker cabs where you had to paint at least 2,000 little black and white squares on each one of them, making sure to follow the roof line, doors, fenders...no...seriously...it was, as you've already guessed...decals!

The original Checker border had, for easier identification, a factory part number for every piece and each one could be ordered individually or as a 15-piece kit with 7 curved parts for the roof and 8 straight pieces for the belt line.

On the back of this original Checker border sticker, you can clearly see the part number and position on the car: #646060—Front Fender Horizontal. The width of the checkerboard is 2.5 inches.

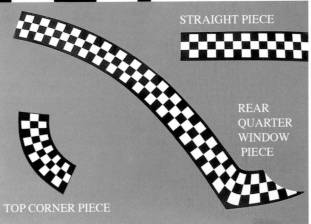

STRAIGHT PIECE

REAR QUARTER WINDOW PIECE

TOP CORNER PIECE

Taxi Medallions

One would think that the most expensive part of a taxicab could be the engine, transmission or computerized ignition but that would be wrong. The most expensive part of most taxis is the operating medallion! The medallion gaurantees that the taxicab is officially licensed by a city and isn't a bandit cab. As an example, an individual medallion to operate a cab in NYC costs approximately $350,000. The best way to recognize a Manhattan medallion taxi is to look at the hood for a metal, stamped plate bearing the 4 digit numbers of the taxi (one number, one letter and two numbers). Every year, the shape of the plate changes. The New York TLC (Taxi and Limousine Commission) controls the licensed taxicabs and their number is limited at 11,500. Other cities also have medallions, which can appear as metal plates or window stickers.

"Licensed taxicab". Car shaped NYC medallion from the mid-1980s.

The most sought after one! "Licensed Taxicab"—The "Big Apple" shaped NYC medallion (circa 1978).

2000 "Licensed Hackney Carriage" from Boston. Usually found on the front of the taxicab.

1997-1998. Licensed Taxicab. A very colorful medallion just loaded with symbols of New York City: Checker cab, Lower Manhattan skyline, Brooklyn Bridge and the twin towers of the World Trade Center.

2003 "Licensed taxicab". Our troops are in Iraq, this medallion is a tribute that proudly adorns 11.500 cabs in New York City.

1970 "Public Vehicle License" Chicago taxi medallion.

Miniature Taxis

There are countless miniature taxicabs available on the enthusiast market. Since the first motorized cabs appeared on the streets of major cities, toy and model manufacturers have been making taxis for kids and collectors to enjoy with different scales, materials, features and colors to imitate the real thing. The many different colors used to attract adult fares seem to stimulate young minds, as well. We've decided to show just a few fine examples and we suggest for those interested in learning more, to refer to the numerous books available on that subject.

1981 Checker Cab, City of Chicago, from Sunstar (1/18 scale).

1940 Packard taxi from Rextoys (1/43 scale).

1981 Checker Cab, City of Los Angeles, from Sunstar (1/18 scale).

1946 DeSoto Skyview from the Sun Motor Co. (1/43 scale). Note that sun roof, passengers and luggage rack have been added on this model.

1981 Checker Cab, City of New York, from Sunstar (1/18 scale). (Note: there is another Checker cab in that series, not featured here: City of Atlanta, yellow and white.)

1949 Checker New York Yellow Cab from Brooklin Models Ltd., of England. A beautiful detailed diecast model (1/43 scale).

1900 Meier Hansom cab horse drawn taxi (Penny Toy), 4 inches long.

1924 Arcade cast iron Yellow Cab bank with driver (8 inches long).

1926 Arcade cast iron Yellow Cab with driver (Beltline version; 8 inches long).

1927 Strauss, green Checker cab (Tin Toy) 8 inches long.

1927 Nonpareil Checker cab (Tin Toy), 6 inches long. Rare version with checker board and rear doors logo.

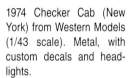

1953 Checker cab model A6, from Victory models, "La familia" series. Made of resin (1/43 scale). One of the best detailed 1950s Checker model ever produced.

1974 Checker Cab (New York) from Western Models (1/43 scale). Metal, with custom decals and headlights.

1949 Checker, New York National Transportation cab from Brooklin Models Ltd. of England. Another beautiful detailed diecast model (1/43 scale).

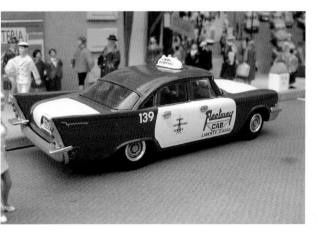

1957 DeSoto Firesweep Fleetway cab from Western Models. Metal (1/43 scale).

Taxi Memorabilia

We made a small selection to give you an idea of what is around. With the advent of the internet and sites like "Ebay.com", a lot of taxi memorabilia is now for sale and garages and attics are clearing out.

A cardboard advertisement for the movie "The Yellow Cab Man" (1950). At that time, cabs in the Los Angeles area had special frames mounted in the passenger compartment for advertising, motion picture publicity, etc... (size about 11 inches long).

1922 Checker Cab Grille Emblem with enamel vintage logo. This heavy piece of brass was turned into a paperweight later on.

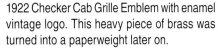

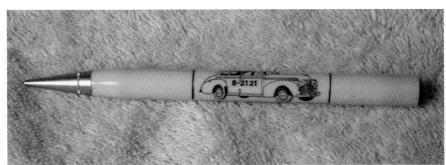

Yellow Cab advertising pens circa 1940.

Grand 5000 Taxi "Yellow Cab Co. of Kansas City" Ink blotter. Circa 1928 (9 in. x 4 in.).

Another nice taxi item: a rare 1920s taxicab coin purse shaped like a taxi hat. Made of leather and metal. Nice drawing of a lady entering a cab molded into the lid of the purse (3 inches wide and 1½ inches high).

A very cute 1920s Valentine card showing the back of a Yellow Cab (open and closed) that says: "If you want me for a fellow, just try this in a yellow" (size 6½" x 5").

1975 Checker Cab metal belt buckle from Chicago Yellow Cab Co.

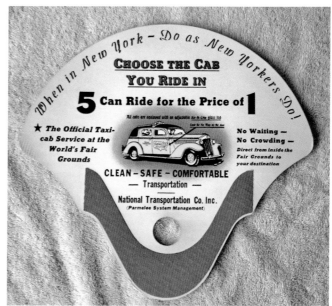

1939 New York World's Fair Yellow Cab fan advertising for National Transportation Co. Inc (Part of Parmelee System management). The cabs, Checker models Y, were all equiped with the Air-N-lite glass top.

THE ONE TAXI LOLA, GORBIE, SANTA, DRAC...AND OPERATORS EVERYWHERE ARE HAILING!

From the #1 pinball company in the world, only TAXI has its meter running . . . collecting fare after fare after fare at locations everywhere! And why is TAXI such a powerhouse when it comes to profits? Because Williams' quality, dependability and proven play appeal make TAXI *the* pinball joyride of a lifetime!

Williams®
ELECTRONICS GAMES, INC.

1988 Williams "TAXI " Electronic Pinball. Note that the rooflight is molded after one of the famous "Waters" lights from the 1940s.

Taxis in the Movies

There are countless movies with taxicabs as co-stars. Since the beginning of the motion picture business, taxicabs have played in more movies than any famous actor could claim. Next time you watch an older film, try to spot the cab and see what it is...Here are some examples:

One of the most well known cab drivers of all time, Robert De Niro starred in Martin Scorcese's 1976 masterpiece, *Taxi Driver*, also starring Jodie Foster. The cab was a typical New York Checker A11 of the mid 1970s.

A card from the 1950 hit movie, *The Yellow Cab Man*. This MGM motion picture was shot in black and white and color was added later on the lobby cards for additional attractiveness (Note that they painted Red Skelton's left hand yellow!).

Baby's Day Out, a 1994 Motion picture from 20th Century Fox, starring Joe Mantegna and Lara Flynn Boyle. During the journey, a Checker cab helps baby Bink escape from three kidnappers.

The 1953 movie, *Taxi,* starred Dan Dayley and Constance Smith. Co-star in that movie: A 1948 DeSoto Skyview taxi.

Dan Dayley in *Taxi*, a 1953 release from 20th Century Fox, standing by his '48 DeSoto "Skyview" cab. (Note the 1951 license plate starting by the "O" prefix for the Taxi series). This is a privately owned cab which explains why it is in such good shape after 5 years on the streets of New York City.

Actor Sid Melton in the 1951 movie, *Stop That Cab*. Interesting still photo of Sid wearing the typical Yellow Cab hat, driving a DeSoto cab with partition, Ohmer meter and James Waters Yellow rooflight. It is obvious that this old cab became a Hollywood prop as they removed the windshield to avoid glare while filming Sid at the wheel.

James Gleason, starring in the 1950 movie hit, *The Yellow Cab Man*, has the old fashion cabbie look with suit, tie and his tilted hat.

May 1, 1941, Orson Welles, coming out of a Bell cab at the premiere of *Citizen Kane*. The cab is a model A Checker with interesting roof lamps shaped like bells.

On the Town, 1949 MGM musical also starred a 1948 DeSoto Skyview from the Globe Cab Co. with moon roof, jump seats, partition and bucket seat for the driver. Betty Garrett, the cab driver, asks Frank Sinatra, a sailor, to sit by her in the luggage compartment next to the meter. How uncomfortable! But who could say no to "Brunhilde 'Hilde' Esterhazy", the man-chasing taxi driver? Also starring Gene Kelly, Anne Miller, Jules Munshin and Vera Ellen.

Betty Garrett is a taxi driver for the Globe Cab Co. in the 1949 MGM musical, *On the Town*, also starring Frank Sinatra.

Marilyn Monroe posed for photographers as she stepped out of an A8 Checker cab in New York circa 1957. It's not uncommon for celebrities to travel incognito in taxis.

Ginger Rogers and Joseph Cotten in the 1944 movie, *I'll be Seeing You.* Another DeSoto cab, most likely a 1941, can be spotted because of its recognizable lights above the rear doors.

Mickey Mouse at the wheel of a 1981 Checker cab! Two American icons! (Courtesy of Disney© *photo by Chris Monier 2005*)

More Great Titles From

Iconografix

More great books from **Iconografix**

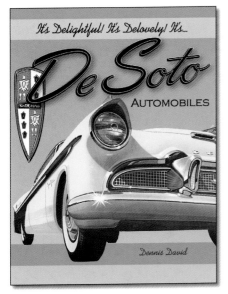

ISBN 1-58388-172-7

ISBN 1-58388-167-0

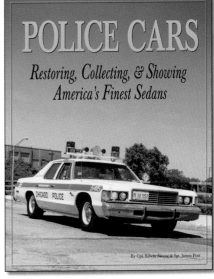

ISBN 1-58388-046-1

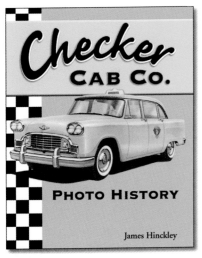

ISBN 1-58388-100-X

Iconografix, Inc.
P.O. Box 446, Dept BK,
Hudson, WI 54016
For a free catalog call:
1-800-289-3504
info@iconografixinc.com
www.iconografixinc.com

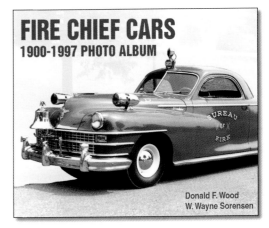

ISBN 1-882256-87-5

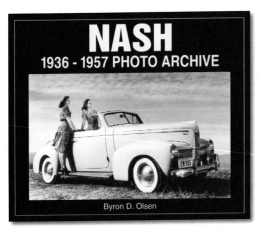

ISBN 1-58388-086-0

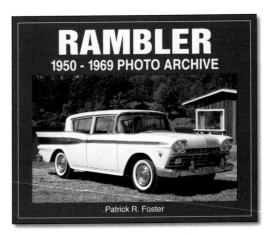

ISBN 1-58388-078-X